HITLER'S WAR MACHINE

PANZERS I & II
GERMANY'S LIGHT TANKS

EDITED AND INTRODUCED BY
BOB CARRUTHERS

Pen & Sword
MILITARY

This edition published in 2013 by
Pen & Sword Military
An imprint of
Pen & Sword Books Ltd
47 Church Street
Barnsley
South Yorkshire
S70 2AS

First published in Great Britain in 2012 in digital format by
Coda Books Ltd.

Copyright © Coda Books Ltd, 2012
Published under licence by Pen & Sword Books Ltd.

ISBN 978 1 78159 209 0

A CIP catalogue record for this book is
available from the British Library

Printed and bound by
CPI Group (UK) Ltd, Croydon, CR0 4YY

Pen & Sword Books Ltd incorporates the Imprints of Pen & Sword Aviation, Pen &
Sword Family History, Pen & Sword Maritime, Pen & Sword Military, Pen &
Sword Discovery, Pen & Sword Politics, Pen & Sword Atlas, Pen & Sword
Archaeology, Wharncliffe Local History, Wharncliffe True Crime, Wharncliffe
Transport, Pen & Sword Select, Pen & Sword Military Classics, Leo Cooper, The
Praetorian Press, Claymore Press, Remember When, Seaforth Publishing and
Frontline Publishing

For a complete list of Pen & Sword titles please contact
PEN & SWORD BOOKS LIMITED
47 Church Street, Barnsley, South Yorkshire, S70 2AS, England
E-mail: enquiries@pen-and-sword.co.uk
Website: www.pen-and-sword.co.uk

CONTENTS

Introduction 4

Section 1: The Panzer I...9

Section 2: The Panzer II 25

Section 3: Legion Condor...40

Section 4: Contemporary Documents.....................................61

More from the Same Series 86

INTRODUCTION

THIS BOOK forms part of the series entitled 'Hitler's War Machine.' The aim is to provide the reader with a varied range of materials drawn from original writings covering the strategic, operational and tactical aspects of the weapons and battles of Hitler's war. The concept behind the series is to provide the well-read and knowledgeable reader with an interesting compilation of related primary sources combined with the best of what is in the public domain to build a picture of a particular aspect of that titanic struggle.

I am pleased to report that the series has been well received and it is a pleasure to be able to bring original primary sources to the attention of an interested readership. I particularly enjoy discovering new primary sources, and I am pleased to be able to present them unadorned and unvarnished to a sophisticated audience. The primary sources such as Die Wehrmacht and Signal, speak for themselves and the readership I strive to serve is the increasingly well informed community of reader/historians which needs no editorial lead and can draw its own conclusions. I am well aware that our community is constantly striving to discover new nuggets of information, and I trust that with this volume I have managed to stimulate fresh enthusiasm and that at least some of these facts and articles will be new to you and will provoke readers to research further down these lines of investigation, and perhaps cause established views to be challenged once more. I am aware at all times in compiling these materials that our relentless pursuit of more and better historical information is at the core our common passion. I trust that this selection will contribute to that search and will help all of us to better comprehend and understand the bewildering events of the last century.

In order to produce an interesting compilation giving a flavour of events at the tactical and operational level I have returned once more to the wartime US Intelligence series of pamphlets, which contain an intriguing series of contemporary articles on weapons and tactics. I find this series of pamphlets particularly fascinating as they are written in, what was then, the present tense and, as such, provide us with a sense of what was happening at the face of battle as events unfolded.

The first vehicle to be produced in any numbers for the Panzerwaffe was, of course, the tiny Panzer I, which at the time was known as the MG Panzerwagen. Delivery of 318 of these had been made by August 1935, along with 15 of the Zugfuhrerwagen, which was later to become the Panzer III. One aspect of tank design which the Germans got absolutely right from the very outset was to identify the importance of radio communications. Although initially only the command tanks were fitted with radios that could both transmit and receive, the other vehicles were at last equipped with receiving radio sets,

A Panzer I in action during the Spanish Civil War

A Panzer II in flames following a hit near Tobruk 1941.

and this was a major advance upon the thinking of many of the countries which would come to oppose Germany. Throughout 1934 exercises continued with the experimental tank units and a number of other valuable lessons quickly became apparent, particularly the need for close co-operation between the air forces and the tanks on the ground. At this point the first serious tank tactics which were to bring so much success during the Second World War began to appear. It was soon obvious that the tanks needed to be employed on a relatively narrow front. A divisional front was estimated at about three kilometres, a great change from the wide fronts of the Great War. It was still obvious to the German High Command that the decisions which were being made, were based on theory, rather than practice. Germany - and indeed every other nation of the time - had no practical experience to draw upon, therefore a number of educated guesses were made.

In January 1936 General Beck reported to the High Command, his findings being based on a study of a French organisation. He was also very critical of the slow rise in production capacity which was hampering the development of the tank force. Interestingly, the debate about which tasks tanks were suitable for, and whether specialist machines had to be developed for each task, was already beginning to take shape. Beck's report clearly stated that the three main tasks of the Panzers were supporting infantry, operating in units with other mobile weapons and, finally, combating other tanks. Beck himself was unable to come to a decision about whether a single tank should be developed with the capability to take on each of these purposes or whether a specialist vehicle should he designed for each purpose.

Ultimately the decision was that the light tanks would be used in a scouting role and that an infantry support tank would be developed which was later to come to fruition in the form of the Panzer IV; this decision cast the Panzer III in the role of main battle tank. Amazingly the decision was taken that the 3.7cm gun which initially equipped the Panzer III would be sufficient for the battle conditions. The various types of German tank design were to cater for most eventualities on the battlefield. Initially the Panzer I was considered to be fit for training purposes only, however manufacturing proceeded very slowly and eventually both the Panzer I and II were earmarked for the reconnaissance role. The Panzer III was essentially designed for break-through and anti-tank operations and the Panzer IV was designed to provide close support for the infantry battling their way forward against dug-In positions. Almost from the outset the limitations of the design for the Panzer I were obvious. The armament in the form of two machine guns, was inadequate for most purposes on the battlefield. In addition the very thin armour gave protection only against rifle bullets: almost any battlefield weapon could penetrate the armour. More significant was the fact that the crew was comprised of only two men.

In October 1935 General Liese, head of the Heere's Waffenamt issued a report which gave the limitations of the tanks. He noted that the MG Panzerwagen (Panzer I), although fitted out only with two 7.9mm machine guns, could be adapted to attack armoured cars and other light tanks if it was issued with special S.M.P. steel core ammunition. In the case of the MG Panzer II, it was noted that the muzzle velocity of the 2cm gun could penetrate up to 10mm of armoured plate at a range of up to 700 metres. It was therefore decided that the Panzer II could engage armoured cars with success, and was also fully functional for combat against tanks with approximately the same armour as itself. Liese noted that the tanks most likely to be encountered in large numbers in a war against the French were the light Renault Ml7 and Ml8 tanks, of which there were about three thousand operational in the French forces at the time. It was also thought that the Panzer II would be the equal of the Renault NC37 and NC31 tanks. Against the heavier French tanks, including the Char B, it was noted that the Panzer II was practically worthless. Despite these reservations large-scale delivery of the Panzer II was already in train and was expected to commence from 1st April 1937.

The Panzer I actually entered active service in 1937 with the Legion Condor and proved to be an efficient machine within its highly proscribed limits. There are those who state that the Panzer II was also deployed in Spain although I can find no evidence to support this claim. Perhaps there Is someone out there who can resolve the debate, for the time being I continue to err on the side of caution

Thank you for buying this volume in the series we hope you will enjoy discovering some new insights you will go on to try the others in the series.

Bob Carruthers
Edinburgh 2012

THE PANZER I

THE PANZER I was a light tank produced in Germany in the 1930s. The name is short for the German Panzerkampfwagen I (armored fighting vehicle mark I), abbreviated PzKpfw I. The tank's official German ordnance inventory designation was SdKfz 101 (special purpose vehicle 101).

Design of the Panzer I began in 1932 and mass production in 1934. Intended only as a training tank to introduce the concept of armored warfare to the German Army, the Panzer I saw combat in Spain during the Spanish Civil War, in Poland, France, the Soviet Union and North Africa during the Second World War, and in China during the Second Sino-Japanese War. Experiences with the Panzer I during the Spanish Civil War helped shape the German armored corps' invasion of Poland in 1939 and France in 1940. By 1941, the Panzer I chassis design was used for production of tank destroyers and assault guns. There were attempts to upgrade the Panzer I throughout its service history, including those foreign nations who had been equipped with the Panzer I, to extend the design lifespan. It continued to serve in the armed forces of Spain until 1954.

The Panzer I's performance in combat was limited by its thin armor and light armament of two general purpose machine guns. As a design intended for training, the Panzer I was not as capable as other light tanks of the era, such as the Soviet T-26. Although weak in combat, it nonetheless formed a large portion of Germany's tank strength in numbers and was used in all major campaigns between September 1939 and December 1941. The

Testing the capabilities of a Panzer I

small, vulnerable light tank would be surpassed in importance by better-known German tanks such as the Panzer IV, Panther, and Tiger. Nevertheless, the Panzer I's contribution to the early victories of Nazi Germany during the Second World War was significant.

Development history

The post-World War I Treaty of Versailles of 1919 prohibited the design, manufacture and deployment of tanks within the Reichswehr. Paragraph Twenty-four of the treaty provided for a 100,000-mark fine and imprisonment of up to six months for anybody who manufactured armoured vehicles, tanks or similar machines, which may be turned to military use.

Despite the manpower and technical limitations imposed upon the German Army by the Treaty of Versailles, several Reichswehr officers established a clandestine General Staff to study the lessons which could be learned from World War I and develop future strategies and tactics accordingly. Although at first the concept of the tank as a mobile weapon of war met with apathy, German industry was silently encouraged to look into tank design, while quiet cooperation was undertaken with the Soviet Union at KAMA. There was also minor military cooperation with Sweden, including the extraction of technical data that proved invaluable to early German tank design. As early as 1926 various German companies, including Rheinmetall and Daimler-Benz, produced a single prototype armed with a large 75-millimeter cannon (the Großtraktor, "large tractor", was so codenamed to veil the true purpose of the vehicle). Only two years later prototypes of the new Leichttraktor ("light tractor"), were produced by German companies, armed with 37-millimeter KwK L/45 guns. The Großtraktor was later put into service for a brief period with the 1 Panzer Division; the Leichttraktor remained in testing until 1935.

In the late 1920s and early 1930s German tank theory was pioneered by two figures: General Oswald Lutz and his chief of staff, Lieutenant Colonel Heinz Guderian. Guderian became the more influential of the two and his ideas were widely publicized. Like his contemporary Sir Percy Hobart, Guderian initially envisioned an armored corps (panzerkorps) composed of several types of tanks. This included a slow infantry tank, armed with a small-caliber cannon and several machine guns. The infantry tank, according to Guderian, was to be heavily armored to defend against enemy anti-tank guns and artillery. He also envisioned a fast breakthrough tank, similar to the British cruiser tank, which was to be armored against enemy anti-tank weapons and have a large 75-millimeter (2.95 in) main gun. Lastly, Germany would need a heavy tank, armed with a massive 150-millimeter (5.9 in) cannon to defeat enemy fortifications, and even stronger armor. Such a tank would require a weight of 70 to 100 tonnes and was completely impractical given the manufacturing capabilities of the day.

Soon after rising to power in Germany, Adolf Hitler approved the creation of Germany's first panzer divisions. Simplifying his earlier proposal, Guderian suggested the design of a main combat vehicle which would be developed into the Panzer III, and a breakthrough tank, the Panzer IV. No existing design appealed to Guderian. As a stopgap, the German Army ordered a preliminary vehicle to train German tank crews. This became the Panzer I.

The Panzer I's design history can be traced to 1932's Landwirtschaftlicher Schlepper (La S) (Agricultural Tractor) armored fighting vehicle. The La S was intended not just to train Germany's panzer troops, but to prepare Germany's industry for the mass production of tanks in the near future: a difficult engineering feat for the time. In July 1932, Krupp revealed a prototype of the Landswerk Krupp A, or LKA, with a sloped front glacis plate and large central casemate, a design heavily influenced by the British Carden Loyd tankette. The tank was armed with two obsolescent 7.92-millimeter (.312 in) MG-13 Dreyse machine guns. Machine guns were known to be largely useless against even the lightest tank armor of the time, restricting the Panzer I to a training and anti-infantry role by design.

A mass-produced version of the LKA was designed by a collaborative team from Daimler-Benz, Henschel, Krupp, MAN, and Rheinmetall, exchanging the casemate for a rotating turret. This version was accepted into service after testing in 1934. Although these tanks were referred to as the La S and LKA well beyond the start of production, its official designation, assigned in 1938, was Panzerkampfwagen I Ausführung. A ('model A' or, more accurately, 'batch A'). The first fifteen tanks, produced between February and March 1934, did not include the rotating turret and were used for crew training. Following these, production was switched to the combat version of the tank. The Ausf. A was under-armored, with steel plate of only 13 millimeters (0.51 in) at its thickest. The tank had several design flaws, including suspension problems which made the vehicle pitch at high speed, and engine overheating. The driver was positioned inside the chassis and used conventional steering levers to control the tank, while the commander was positioned in the turret where he also acted as gunner. The two crewmen

PzKpfw I Ausf. F on display at the Belgrade Military Museum

could communicate by means of a voice tube. Machine gun ammunition was stowed in five bins, containing various numbers of 25-round magazines. Author Lucas Molina Franco states that 833 Panzerkampfwagen I Ausf. A tanks were built in total, Terry Gander assesses the number 818 units while Bryan Perrett estimates the number may have been as low as low as 300.

Many of the problems in the Ausf. A were corrected with the introduction of the Ausf. B. The engine was replaced by the water-cooled, six-cylinder Maybach NL 38 TR, developing 98 horsepower (73 kW), and the gearbox was changed to a more reliable model. The larger engine required the extension of the vehicle's chassis by 40 cm (16 in), and this allowed the improvement of the tank's suspension, adding an additional bogie wheel and raising the tensioner. The tank's weight increased by 0.4 tons. Production of the Ausf. B began in August 1935 and finished in early 1937—Franco writes 840 were constructed, but notes that only 675 of these were combat models, while Perrett suggests a total number of 1,500 (offsetting the low number of Ausf. A he proposes) and Gander a total of 675.

A Panzer I crew of the Condor Legion.

The Next Generation

Two more combat versions of the Panzer I were designed and produced between 1939 and 1942. By this stage the design concept had been superseded by medium and heavy tanks and neither variant was produced in sufficient numbers to have a real impact on the progress of the war. These new tanks had nothing in common with either the Ausf. A or B except name. One of these, the Panzer I Ausf. C, was designed jointly between Krauss-Maffei and Daimler-Benz in 1939 to provide an amply armored and armed reconnaissance light tank. The Ausf. C boasted a completely new chassis and turret, a modern torsion-bar suspension and five interleaved roadwheels. It also had a maximum armor thickness of 30 millimeters (1.18 in), over twice that of either the Ausf. A or B, and was armed with a 20-millimeter (0.78 in) EW 141 autocannon. Forty of these tanks were produced, along with six prototypes. Two tanks were deployed to 1 Panzer Division in 1943, and the other thirty-eight were deployed to the LVIII Panzer Reserve Corps during the Normandy landings.

The second vehicle, the Ausf. F, was as different from the Ausf. C as it was from the Ausf. A and B. Intended as an infantry support tank, the Panzer I Ausf. F had a maximum armour thickness of 80 millimeters (3.15 in) and weighed between 18 and 21 tonnes. The Ausf. F was armed with two 7.92-millimeter MG-34s. Thirty were produced in 1940, and a second order of 100 was later canceled. In order to compensate for the increased weight, a new 150 horsepower (110 kW) Maybach HL45 Otto engine was used, allowing a maximum road speed of 25 kilometers per hour (15.5 mph). Eight of the thirty tanks produced were sent to the 1 Panzer Division in 1943 and saw combat at the Battle of Kursk. The rest were given to several army schools for training and evaluation purposes.

Combat history

Spanish Civil War

On 18 July 1936, war broke out on the Iberian Peninsula as Spain dissolved into a state of civil war. After the chaos of the initial uprising, two sides coalesced and began to consolidate their position—the Popular front (the Republicans) and the Spanish Nationalist front. In an early example of a proxy war, both sides quickly received support from other countries, most notably the Soviet Union and Germany, who wanted to test their tactics and equipment. The first shipment of foreign tanks, fifty Soviet T-26's, arrived on 15 October. The shipment was under the surveillance of the German Navy and Germany immediately responded by sending forty-one Panzer I's to Spain a few days later. This first shipment was followed by four more shipments of Panzer I Ausf. B's, with a total of 122 vehicles.

The first shipment of Panzer I's was brought under the command of Lieutenant Colonel Wilhelm Ritter von Thoma in Gruppe Thoma (also referred to as Panzergruppe Drohne). Gruppe Thoma formed part of Gruppe Imker, the ground formations of the German Condor Legion, who fought on the side of Franco's Nationalists. Between July and October, a rapid Nationalist advance from Seville to Toledo placed them in position to take the Spanish capital, Madrid. The Nationalist advance and the fall of the town of Illescas to Nationalist armies on 18 October 1936 caused the government of the Popular Front's Second Republic, including President Manuel Azaña, to flee to Barcelona and Valencia. In an attempt to stem the Nationalist tide and gain crucial time for Madrid's defence, Soviet armor was deployed south of the city under the command of Colonel Krivoshein before the end of October. At this time, several T-26 tanks under the command of Captain Paul Arman were thrown into a Republican counterattack directed towards the town of Torrejon de Velasco in an attempt to cut off the Nationalist advance north. This was the first tank battle in the Spanish Civil War. Despite initial success, poor communication between the Soviet Republican armor and Spanish Republican infantry caused the isolation of Captain Arman's force and the subsequent destruction of a number of tanks. This battle also marked the first use of the molotov cocktail against tanks. Ritter von Thoma's Panzer Is fought for the Nationalists only days later on 30 October, and immediately experienced problems. As the Nationalist armor advanced, it was engaged by the Commune de Paris battalion, equipped with Soviet BA-10 armored cars. The 45-millimeter (1.7 in) gun in the BA-10 was more than sufficient to knock out the poorly armored Panzer I at ranges of over 500 meters (550 yd).

COMPARISON OF LIGHT TANKS IN THE SPANISH CIVIL WAR				
	T-26	Panzer I	CV.33	CV.35
Weight	9.4 t	5.4 t	3.15 t	2.3 t
Gun	45 mm cannon	2 × 7.92 mm MG 13	6.5 mm or 8 mm machine gun	8 mm Breda machine gun
Ammunition	122 rounds	2,250 rounds	3,200 8mm or 3,800 6.5mm	3,200
Road range	175 km	200 km	125 km	125 km
Armor	7–16 mm	7–13 mm	5–15 mm	5–13.5 mm

Although the Panzer I would participate in almost every major Nationalist offensive of the war, the Nationalist army began to deploy more and more captured T-26 tanks to offset their disadvantage in protection and firepower. At one point, von Thoma offered up to 500 pesetas for each T-26 captured. Although the Panzer I was initially able to knock out the T-26 at close range—150 meters (165 yd) or less—using an armor-piercing 7.92 millimeter bullet, the Republican tanks began to engage at ranges where they were immune to the machine guns of the Panzer I.

The Panzer I was upgraded in order to increase its lethality. On 8 August 1937, Major General García Pallasar received a note from Generalísimo Francisco Franco which expressed the need for a Panzer I (or negrillo, as their Spanish crews called them) with a 20-millimeter gun. Ultimately, the piece chosen was the Breda Model 1935, due to the simplicity of the design over competitors such as the German Flak 30. Furthermore, the 20 mm Breda was capable of perforating 40 millimeters of armor at 250 meters (1.57 in at 275 yd), which was more than sufficient to penetrate the frontal armor of the T-26. Although originally forty Italian CV.35 light tanks were ordered with the Breda in place of their original armament, this order was subsequently canceled after it was thought adaptation of the same gun to the Panzer I would yield better results. Prototypes were ready by September 1937 and an order was placed after successful results. The mounting of the Breda in the Panzer I required the original turret to be opened at the top and then extended by a vertical supplement. Four of these tanks were finished at the Armament Factory of Seville, but further production was canceled as it was decided sufficient numbers of Republican T-26 tanks had been captured to fulfill the Nationalist leadership's request for more lethal tanks. The Breda modification was not particularly liked by German crews, as the unprotected gap in the turret, designed to allow the tank's commander to aim, was found to be a dangerous weak point.

In late 1938, another Panzer I was sent to the Armament Factory of Seville in order to mount a 45 mm gun, captured from a Soviet tank (a T-26 or BT-5). A second was sent sometime later in order to exchange the original armament for a 37-millimeter Maklen anti-tank gun, which had been deployed to Asturias in late 1936 on the Soviet ship A. Andreiev. It remains unknown to what extent these trials and adaptations were completed, although it is safe to assume neither adaptation was successful beyond the drawing board.

PANZER I DELIVERIES TO SPAIN (1936–1939)	
Date	Number of Vehicles
October 1936*	41
Dec-36	21
Aug-37	30
End of 1937	10
Jan-39	30
Total:	122

Formed part of the Condor Legion

Second World War

During the initial campaigns of the Second World War, Germany's light tanks, including the Panzer I, formed the bulk of its armored strength. In March 1938, the German Army marched into Austria, experiencing a mechanical breakdown rate of up to thirty percent. However, the experience revealed to Guderian several faults within the German Panzerkorps and he subsequently improved logistical support. In October 1938, Germany occupied Czechoslovakia's Sudetenland, and the remainder of the country in March 1939. The capture of Czechoslovakia allowed several Czech tank designs, such as the Panzer 38(t), and their subsequent variants and production, to be incorporated into the German Army's strength. It also prepared German forces for the invasion of Poland.

A Panzer I Ausf B on the streets of Calais, France in May 1940, while rounding up British prisoners of war.

Poland and the campaign in the west

On 1 September 1939, Germany invaded Poland using seventy-two divisions (including 16 reserve infantry divisions in OKH reserves), including seven panzer divisions (1., 2., 3., 4., 5., 10., "Kempf") and four light divisions (1., 2., 3., 4.). Three days later, France and Britain declared war on Germany. The seven panzer and four light divisions were arrayed in five armies, forming two army groups. The battalion strength of the 1 Panzer Division included no less than fourteen Panzer Is, while the other six divisions included thirty-four. A total of about 2,700 tanks were available for the invasion of Poland, but only 310 of the heavier Panzer III and IV tanks were available. Furthermore, 350 were of Czech design—the rest were either Panzer Is or Panzer IIs. The invasion was swift and the last Polish pockets of resistance surrendered on 6 October. The entire campaign had lasted five weeks (with help of the Soviet forces which attacked on 17 September), and the success of Germany's tanks in the campaign was summed up in response to Hitler on 5 September: when

Panzer I Ausf. A in combat during the German invasion of Norway.

asked if it had been the dive bombers who destroyed a Polish artillery regiment, Guderian replied, "No, our panzers!"

The Poles suffered almost 190,000 casualties (including around 66,300 killed) in the campaign, the Germans around 55,000 (including around 35,000 wounded. However, some 832 tanks (including 320 PzI, 259 PzII, 40 Pz III, 76 PzIV, 77 Pz35(t), 13 PzBef III, 7 PzBef 38(t), 34 other PzBef and some Pz38(t)) were lost during the campaign, approximately 341 of which were never to return to service. This represented about a third of Germany's armor deployed for the Polish campaign. During the campaign no less than a half of Germany's tanks were unavailable due to maintenance issues or enemy action, and of all tanks, the Panzer I proved the most vulnerable to Polish anti-tank weapons.

Furthermore, it was found that handling of armored forces during the campaign left much to be desired. During the beginning of Guderian's attack in northern Poland, his corps was held back to coordinate with infantry for quite a while, preventing a faster advance. It was only after Army Group South had its attention taken from Warsaw at the Battle of Bzura that

Guderian's armor was fully unleashed. There were still lingering tendencies to reserve Germany's armor, even if in independent divisions, to cover an infantry advance or the flanks of advancing infantry armies. Although tank production was increased to 125 tanks per month after the Polish Campaign, losses forced the Germans to draw further strength from Czech tank designs, and light tanks continued to form the majority of Germany's armored strength.

Months later, Panzer Is participated in Operation Weserübung—the invasion of Denmark and Norway.

Despite its obsolescence, the Panzer I was also used in the invasion of France in May 1940. Of 2,574 tanks available for the campaign, no fewer than 523 were Panzer Is. Furthermore, there were only 627 Panzer IIIs and IVs. At least a fifth of Germany's armor was composed of Panzer Is, while almost four-fifths was light tanks of one type or another, including 955 Panzer II, 106 Czech Panzer 35(t), and 228 Panzer 38(t). For their defense, the French boasted up to 4,000 tanks, including 300 Char B1, armed with a 47-millimeter (1.7 in) gun in the turret and a larger 75-millimeter (2.95 in) low-velocity gun in the hull. The French also had around 250 Somua S-35, widely regarded as one of the best tanks of the period, armed with the same 47 millimeter main gun and protected by almost 55 millimeters (2.17 in) of armor at its thickest point. Nevertheless, the French also deployed over 3,000 light tanks, including about 500 World War I-vintage FT-17s. The two main advantages German armor enjoyed were radios allowing them to coordinate faster than their British or French counterparts and superior tactical doctrine.

North Africa and campaigns in the east

Italian setbacks in Egypt and their colony of Libya caused Hitler to dispatch aircraft to Sicily, and a blocking force to North Africa. This blocking force was put under the command of

Panzerbefehlswagen in Russia.

Lieutenant General Erwin Rommel and included the motorized 5th Light Division and the 15th Panzer Division. This force landed at Tunis on 12 February 1941. Upon arrival, Rommel had around 150 tanks, about half Panzer III and IV. The rest were Panzer I's and IIs, although the Panzer I was soon replaced. On 6 April 1941, Germany attacked both Yugoslavia and Greece, with fourteen divisions invading Greece from neighboring Bulgaria, which by then had joined the Tripartite Pact. The invasion of Yugoslavia included no less than six panzer divisions, which still fielded the Panzer I. Yugoslavia surrendered 17 April 1941, and Greece fell on 30 April 1941.

The final major campaign in which the Panzer I formed a large portion of the armored strength was Operation Barbarossa, 22 June 1941. The 3,300 German tanks included about 410 Panzer I's. By the end of the month, a large portion of the Red Army found itself trapped in the Minsk pocket, and by 21 September Kiev had fallen, thereby allowing the Germans to concentrate on their ultimate objective, Moscow. Despite the success of Germany's armor in the Soviet Union, between June and September most German officers were shocked to find their tanks were inferior to newer Soviet models, the T-34 and Kliment Voroshilov (KV) series. Army Group North quickly realized that none of the tank guns currently in use by German armor could penetrate the thick armor of the KV-1. The performance of the Red Army during the Battle of Moscow and the growing numbers of new Soviet tanks made it obvious the Panzer I was not suitable for this front. Some less battle-worthy Panzer I's were tasked with towing lorries through mud to alleviate logistics problems at the front.

Foreign service

After Germany, Spain fielded the largest number of Panzer I tanks. A total of 122 were exported to Spain during the Spanish Civil War, and, as late as 1945, Spain's Brunete Armored Division fielded 93. The Panzer I remained in use in Spain until aid arrived from the United States in 1954 when they were replaced by the relatively modern M47 Patton. Between 1935 and 1936, an export version of the Panzer I Ausf. B, named the L.K.B. (Leichte Kampfwagen B), was designed for export to Bulgaria. Modifications included up-gunning to a 20-millimeter gun and fitting a Krupp M 311 V-8 gasoline engine. Although three examples were built, none were exported to Bulgaria, although a single Panzer I Ausf. A had previously been sold. In 1937, around ten Ausf. As were sold to China during a period of Sino-German cooperation, which were used in the Battle of Nanjing by the 3rd Armored Battalion. A final order was supplied to Hungary in 1942, totalling eight Ausf. B's and six command versions. These were incorporated into the 1st Armored Division and saw combat in late 1942.

Variants

Between 1934 and the mid 1940s several variants of the Panzer I were designed, especially during the later years of its combat history. Because they were obsolescent from their introduction, incapable of defeating foreign armor, and outclassed by newer

German tanks, the Panzer I chassis were increasingly repurposed as tank destroyers and other variants. One of the most well known variants was the kleiner Panzerbefehlswagen ("small armored command vehicle"), built on the Ausf. A and Ausf. B chassis—200 of these were manufactured. The Panzer I Ausf. B chassis was also used to build the German Army's first tracked tank destroyer, the Panzerjäger I. This vehicle was armed with a Czech 47-millimeter (1.85 in) anti-tank gun.

PANZER II

THE PANZER II was the common name for a family of German tanks used in World War II. The official German designation was Panzerkampfwagen II (abbreviated PzKpfw II). Although the vehicle had originally been designed as a stopgap while more advanced tanks were developed, it nonetheless went on to play an important role in the early years of World War II, during the Polish and French campaigns. By the end of 1942 it had been largely removed from front line service, and production of the tank itself ceased by 1943. Its chassis remained in use as the basis of several other armored vehicles.

History

In 1934, delays in the design and production of the Panzer III and Panzer IV tanks were becoming apparent. Designs for a stopgap tank were solicited from Krupp, MAN, Henschel, and Daimler-Benz. The final design was based on the Panzer I, but larger, and with a turret mounting a 20 mm anti-tank gun.

The Panzer II

The Marder III was a highly effective tank killer created from the chassis of the Panzer II.

Production began in 1935, but it took another eighteen months for the first combat-ready tank to be delivered.

The Panzer II was the most numerous tank in the German Panzer divisions beginning with the invasion of France, until it was supplemented by the Panzer III and IV in 1940/41. Afterwards, it was used to great effect as a reconnaissance tank.

The Panzer II was used in the German campaigns in Poland, France, the Low Countries, Denmark, Norway, North Africa and the Eastern Front. After being removed from front-line duty, it was used for training and on secondary fronts. The chassis was used for a number of self-propelled guns including the Wespe and Marder II.

Design

Armor

The Panzer II was designed before the experience of the Spanish Civil War of 1936-39 showed that shell-proof armor was required for tanks to survive on a modern battlefield. Prior to that, armor was designed to stop machine gun fire and High Explosive shell fragments.

The Panzer II A, B, and C had 14 mm of slightly sloped homogenous steel armor on the sides, front, and back, with 10 mm of armor on the top and bottom. Many IIC were given increased armor in the front. Starting with the D model, the front armor was increased to 30 mm. The Model F had 35 mm front armour and 20 mm side armor.

This armor could be penetrated by towed antitank weapons such as the Soviet 45mm and French canon de 25 and canon de 47.

Armament

Most tank versions of the Panzer II were armed with a 2 cm KwK 30 55 calibers long cannon. Some later versions used the 2 cm KwK 38 L/55 which was similar. This cannon was based on the 2 cm FlaK 30 anti-aircraft gun, and was capable of firing at a rate of 600 rounds per minute (280 rounds per minute sustained). The Panzer II also had a 7.92 mm Maschinengewehr 34 machine gun mounted coaxially with the main gun.

The 2 cm cannon proved to be ineffective against many Allied tanks, and experiments were made towards replacing it with a 37 mm cannon, but nothing came of this. Prototypes were built with a 50 mm tank gun, but by then the Panzer II had outlived its usefulness as a tank regardless of armament. Greater success was had by replacing the standard armor-piercing explosive ammunition with tungsten cored solid ammunition, but due to material shortages this ammunition was in chronically short supply.

Later development into a self-propelled gun carriage saw the mounting of a 5 cm PaK 38 antitank gun, but this was seen as insufficient for the time, and the larger 7.62 cm PaK 36(r) was installed as an effective stop-gap. The main production antitank version was fitted with a 7.5 cm PaK 40 which was very effective. Artillery mounting began with a few 15 cm sIG 33 heavy infantry guns, but most effective was the 10.5 cm leFH 18, for which the Panzer II chassis became the primary carriage for the war. Most of these versions retained a pintle mounted 7.92 mm MG34 machine gun for defense against infantry and air attack.

Mobility

All production versions of the Panzer II were fitted with a 140 PS, gasoline-fuelled six-cylinder Maybach HL 62 TRM engine and ZF transmissions. Models A, B, and C had a top speed of 40 km/h (25 mph). Models D and E had a Christie suspension and a better transmission, giving a top road speed of 55 km/h (33 mph) but the cross country speed was much lower than previous models, so the Model F reverted back to the previous leaf spring type suspension. All versions had a range of 200 km (120 mi).

Crew

The Panzer II had a crew of three men. The driver sat in the forward hull. The commander sat in a seat in the turret, and was responsible for aiming and firing the guns, while a loader/radio operator stood on the floor of the tank under the turret.

Variants

Development and limited production models

Panzer II Ausf. a (PzKpfw IIa)

Not to be confused with the later Ausf. A (the sole difference being the capitalization of the letter A), the Ausf. a was the first limited production version of the Panzer II to be built, and was subdivided into three sub-variants. The Ausf. a/1 was initially built with a cast idler wheel with rubber tire, but this was replaced after ten production examples with a welded part. The Ausf. a/2 improved engine access issues. The Ausf. a/3 included improved suspension and engine cooling. In general, the specifications for the Ausf. a models was similar, and a total of 75 were produced from May 1936 to February 1937 by Daimler-Benz and MAN. The Ausf. a was considered the 1 Serie under the LaS 100 name.

A Panzer II with a Panzer I following, on the Western Front, 1940

Specifications

- Crew: 3
- Engine: Maybach HL57TR with 6 gear transmission plus reverse
- Weight: 7.6 tonnes
- Dimensions: 4.38 m(l) x 2.14 m(w) x 1.95 m(h)
- Speed: 40 km/h
- Range: 200 km
- Communications: FuG5 radio
- Primary armament: 2 cm KwK 30 L/55 gun with TZF4 gun sight, turret mounted
- Secondary armament: MG34 7.92 mm machine gun, coaxially mounted
- Ammunition: 180 20 mm and 2,250 7.92 mm carried
- Turret: 360° hand traverse with elevation of +20° and depression to -9.5°
- Armour: 13 mm front, side, and rear; 8 mm top; 5 mm bottom

Panzer II Ausf. b (PzKpfw IIb)

Again, not to be confused with the later Ausf. B, the Ausf. b was

A Panzer II rolls into Austria during the Anschluss.

a second limited production series embodying further developments, primarily a heavy reworking of suspension components resulting in a wider track and a longer hull. Length was increased to 4.76 m but width and height were unchanged. Additionally, a Maybach HL62TR engine was used with new drivetrain components to match. Deck armor for the superstructure and turret roof was increased to 10–12 mm. Total weight increased to 7.9 tonnes. Twenty-five were built by Daimler-Benz and MAN in February and March 1937.

Panzer II Ausf. c (PzKpfw IIc)

As the last of the developmental limited production series of Panzer IIs, the Ausf. c came very close to matching the mass production configuration, with a major change to the suspension with the replacement of the six small road wheels with five larger independently sprung road wheels and an additional return roller bringing that total to four. The tracks were further modified and the fenders widened. Total length was increased to 4.81 m and width to 2.22 m, while height was still about 1.99 m. At least 25 of this model were produced from March through July 1937.

Panzer II Ausf. A (PzKpfw IIA)

The first true production model, the Ausf. A included an armor upgrade to 14.5 mm on all sides, as well as a 14.5 mm floor plate, and an improved transmission. The Ausf. A entered production in July 1937.

Panzer II Ausf. B (PzKpfw IIB)

Introducing only minimal changes to the Ausf. A, the Ausf. B superseded it in production from December 1937.

Panzer II Ausf. C (PzKpfw IIC)

Few minor changes were made in the Ausf. C version, which became the standard production model from June 1938 through April 1940. A total of 1,113 examples of Ausf. c, A, B, and C tanks were built from March 1937 through April 1940 by Alkett, FAMO, Daimler-Benz, Henschel, MAN, MIAG, and Wegmann. These models were almost identical and were used in service interchangeably. This was the most widespread tank version of the Panzer II and performed the majority of the tank's service in the Panzer units during the war. Earlier versions of Ausf. C have rounded hull front, but many vehicles of Ausf. C were up-armored to fight in France. These have extra armors bolted on the turret front and super structure front. Also up-armored

PzKpfw II Ausf. C at the Musée des Blindés

A Panzer II Ausf F lies knocked out in the Western Desert.

versions have angled front hull like that of Ausf.F. Some were also retro-fitted with commander's cupolas.

Panzer II Ausf. F (PzKpfw IIF)

Continuing the conventional design of the Ausf. C, the Ausf. F was designed as a reconnaissance tank and served in the same role as the earlier models. The superstructure front was made from a single piece armor plate with a redesigned visor. Also a dummy visor was placed next to it to reduce anti-tank rifle bullets hitting the real visor. The hull was redesigned with a flat 35 mm plate on its front, and armor of the superstructure and turret were built up to 30 mm on the front with 15 mm to the sides and rear. There was some minor alteration of the suspension and a new commander's cupola as well. Weight was increased to 9.5 tonnes. 524 were built from March 1941 to December 1942 as the final major tank version of the Panzer II series.

Panzer II Ausf. D (PzKpfw IID)

With a completely new Christie suspension with four road

wheels, the Ausf. D was developed as a cavalry tank for use in the pursuit and reconnaissance roles. Only the turret was the same as the Ausf. C model, with a new hull and superstructure design and the use of a Maybach HL62TRM engine driving a seven-gear transmission (plus reverse). The design was shorter (4.65 m) but wider (2.3 m) and taller (2.06 m) than the Ausf. C. Speed was increased to 55 km/h. A total of 143 Ausf. D and Ausf. E tanks were built from May 1938 through August 1939 by MAN, and they served in Poland. They were withdrawn in March 1940 for conversion to other types after proving to have poor off road performance.

Panzer II Ausf. E (PzKpfw IIE)

Similar to the Ausf. D, the Ausf. E improved some small items of the suspension, but was otherwise similar and served alongside the Ausf. D.

Panzer II Ausf. J (PzKpfw IIJ)

Continued development of the reconnaissance tank concept led to the much up-armored Ausf. J, which used the same concept as the PzKpfw IF of the same period, under the experimental designation VK1601. Heavier armor was added, bringing protection up to 80 mm on the front and 50 mm to the sides and rear, with 25 mm roof and floor plates, increasing total weight to 18 tonnes. Equipped with the same Maybach HL45P as the PzKpfw IF, top speed was reduced to 31 km/h. Primary armament was the 2 cm KwK 38 L/55 gun. 22 were produced by MAN between April and December 1942, and seven were issued to the 12th Panzer Division on the Eastern Front.

Panzerkampfwagen II ohne Aufbau

One use for obsolete Panzer II tanks which had their turrets removed for use in fortifications was as utility carriers. A number of chassis not used for conversion to self-propelled guns were instead handed over to the Engineers for use as personnel and equipment carriers.

Panzer II Flamm

Based on the same suspension as the Ausf. D and Ausf. E tank versions, the Flamm (also known as "Flamingo")used a new turret mounting a single MG34 machine gun, and two remotely controlled flamethrowers mounted in small turrets at each front corner of the vehicle. Each flamethrower could cover the front 180° arc, while the turret traversed 360°.

The flamethrowers were supplied with 320 litres of fuel and four tanks of compressed nitrogen. The nitrogen tanks were built into armored boxes along each side of the superstructure. Armor was 30 mm to the front and 14.5 mm to the side and rear, although the turret was increased to 20 mm at the sides and rear.

Total weight was 12 tonnes and dimensions were increased to a length of 4.9 m and width of 2.4 m although it was a bit shorter at 1.85 m tall. A FuG2 radio was carried. Two sub-variants existed: the Ausf. A and Ausf. B which differed only in minor suspension components. One hundred and fifty-five Flamm vehicles were built from January 1940 through March 1942. These were mostly on new chassis but 43 were on used Ausf. D and Ausf. E chassis. The Flamm was deployed in the USSR but was not very successful due to its limited armor, and survivors were soon withdrawn for conversion in December 1941.

5 cm PaK 38 auf Fahrgestell Panzerkampfwagen II

Conceived along the same lines as the Marder II, the 5 cm PaK 38 was an expedient solution to mount the 50 mm antitank gun on the Panzer II chassis. However, the much greater effectiveness of the 75 mm antitank gun made this option less desirable and it is not known how many field modifications were made to this effect.

7.62 cm PaK 36(r) auf Fahrgestell Panzerkampfwagen II Ausf. D (Sd.Kfz. 132)

After a lack of success with conventional and flame tank variants on the Christie chassis, it was decided to use the remaining chassis to mount captured Soviet antitank guns. The hull and suspension was unmodified from the earlier models, but the superstructure was built up to provide a large fighting compartment on top of which was mounted a Soviet 76.2 mm antitank gun, which, while not turreted, did have significant traverse. Only developed as an interim solution, the vehicle was clearly too tall and poorly protected, but had a powerful weapon and was better than what the Germans had at the time.

7.5 cm PaK 40 auf Fahrgestell Panzerkampfwagen II (Marder II) (Sd.Kfz. 131)

While the 7.62 cm PaK 36(r) was a good stopgap measure, the 7.5 cm PaK 40 mounted on the tank chassis of the Ausf. F resulted in a better overall fighting machine. New production amounted to 576 examples from June 1942 to June 1943 as well as the conversion of 75 tanks after new production had stopped. The work was done by Daimler-Benz, FAMO, and MAN. A much improved superstructure for the 7.62 cm mounting was built giving a lower profile. The Marder II became a key piece of equipment and served with the Germans on all fronts through the end of the war.

Leichte Feldhaubitze 18 auf Fahrgestell Panzerkampfwagen II (Wespe)

After the development of the Fahrgestell Panzerkampfwagen II for mounting the sIG 33, Alkett designed a version mounting a 10.5 cm leichte Feldhaubitze 18/2 field howitzer in a built-up superstructure. The Panzer II proved an efficient chassis for this weapon and it became the only widely produced self-propelled 105 mm howitzer for Germany. Between February 1943 and June 1944, 676 were built by FAMO and it served with German forces on all major fronts.

Munitions Selbstfahrlafette auf Fahrgestell Panzerkampfwagen II

To support the Wespe in operation, a number of Wespe chassis were completed without installation of the howitzer, instead

Panzer II Ausf. L in the Musée des Blindés, Saumur.

functioning as ammunition carriers. They carried 90 rounds of 105 mm caliber. 159 were produced alongside the Wespe. These could be converted by installation of the leFH 18 in the field if needed.

Panzerkampfwagen II mit Schwimmkörper

One of Germany's first attempts at developing an amphibious tank, the Schwimmkörper was a device built by Gebr Sachsenberg which consisted of two large pontoons that attached to either side of a Panzer II tank. The tanks were specially sealed and some modification to the engine exhaust and cooling was needed. The pontoons were detachable. The modified tanks were issued to the 18th Panzer Regiment which was formed in 1940. However, with cancellation of Operation Sealion, the plan to invade England, the tanks were used in the conventional manner by the regiment on the Eastern Front.

Panzer II Ausf. L (PzKpfw IIL) "Luchs"

A light reconnaissance tank, the Ausf. L was the only Panzer II design with the overlapping/interleaved road wheels and "slack track" configuration to enter series production, with 100 being built from September 1943 to January 1944 in addition to conversion of the four Ausf. M tanks. Originally given the experimental designation VK 1303, it was adopted under the alternate name Panzerspähwagen II and given the popular name Luchs (Lynx). The Lynx was larger than the Ausf. G in most dimensions (length 4.63 m; height 2.21 m; width 2.48 m). It was equipped with a six speed transmission (plus reverse), and could reach a speed of 60 km/h with a range of 290 km. The FuG12 and FuG Spr a radios were installed, while 330 rounds of 20 mm and 2,250 rounds of 7.92 mm ammunition were carried. Total vehicle weight was 11.8 tonnes.

Limited production, experiments and prototypes

Panzer II Ausf. G (PzKpfw IIG)

The fourth and final suspension configuration used for the Panzer II tanks was the five overlapping road wheel configuration termed Schachtellaufwerk by the Germans. This was used as the basis for the redesign of the Panzer II into a reconnaissance tank with high speed and good off-road performance. The Ausf. G was the first Panzer II to use this configuration, and was developed with the experimental designation VK901. There is no record of the Ausf. G being issued to combat units, and only twelve full vehicles were built from April 1941 to February 1942 by MAN. The turrets were subsequently issued for use in fortifications.

Specifications
- Crew: 3
- Engine: Maybach HL66P driving a five speed transmission (plus reverse)
- Weight: 10.5 tonnes
- Dimensions: length 4.24 m; width 2.38 m; height 2.05 m
- Performance: speed 50 km/h; range 200 km
- Main armament: 7.92x94 mm MG141 automatic rifle, turret mounted with TZF10 sight
- Secondary armament: 7.92 mm MG34 machine gun, coaxially mounted

- Turret: 360° hand traverse
- Armor: 30 mm front, 15 mm sides and rear

Panzer II Ausf. H (PzKpfw IIH)

Given experimental designation VK903, the Ausf. H was intended as the production model of the Ausf. G, with armor for the sides and rear increased to 20 mm and a new four speed transmission (plus reverse) similar to that of the PzKpfw 38(t) nA. Only prototypes were ever completed by the time of cancellation in September 1942.

5 cm PaK 38 auf Panzerkampfwagen II

Planned as a light tank destroyer, the first two prototypes were delivered in 1942 but by then their 50 mm gun was not sufficient and the program was canceled in favor of 75 mm weapons.

Brückenleger auf Panzerkampfwagen II

After failed attempts to use the Panzer I as a chassis for a bridge layer, work moved to the Panzer II, led by Magirus. It is not known how many of these conversions were made, but four were known to have been in service with the 7th Panzer Division in May 1940.

15 cm sIG 33 auf Fahrgestell Panzerkampfwagen II (Sf)

One of the first gun mount variants of the Panzer II design was to emplace a 15 cm sIG 33 heavy infantry gun on a turretless Panzer II chassis. The prototype utilized an Ausf. B tank chassis, but it was quickly realized that it was not sufficient for the mounting. A new, longer chassis incorporating an extra road wheel was designed and built, named the Fahrgestell Panzerkampfwagen II. An open-topped 15 mm thick armored superstructure sufficient against small arms and shrapnel was provided around the gun. This was not high enough to give full protection for the crew while manning the gun, although they were still covered directly to the front by the tall gun shield. Only 12 were built in November and December 1941. These served with the 707th and 708th Heavy Infantry Gun Companies in

North Africa until their destruction in 1943.

Bergepanzerwagen auf Panzerkampfwagen II Ausf. J

A single example of an Ausf. J with a jib in place of its turret was found operating as an armored recovery vehicle. There is no record of an official program for this vehicle.

Panzer Selbstfahrlafette 1c

Developed in prototype form only, this was one of three abortive attempts to use the Panzer II chassis for mounting a 5 cm PaK 38 gun, this time on the chassis of the Ausf. G. Two examples were produced which had similar weight to the tank version, and both were put in front-line service, but production was not undertaken as priority was given to heavier armed models.

Panzer II Ausf. M (PzKpfw IIM)

Using the same chassis as the Ausf. H, the Ausf. M replaced the turret with a larger, open-topped turret containing a 5 cm KwK 39/1 gun. Four were built by MAN in August 1942, but did not see service.

VK1602 Leopard

The VK1602 was intended as a 5 cm KwK39-armed replacement for the Ausf. L, with a Maybach HL157P engine driving an eight speed transmission (plus reverse). While the hull was based on that of the PzKpfw IIJ, it was redesigned after the PzKpfw V Panther, most noticeably with the introduction of fully sloped frontal armor. Two versions were initially planned, a lighter, faster 18 ton variant and a slower, 26 ton vehicle; the former was abandoned at an early stage. Subsequently, work on the first prototype was abandoned when it was determined that the vehicle was under-armed for its weight, and versions of the PzKpfw IV and -V could serve just as well in the reconnaissance role while being more capable of defending themselves. This vehicle never received an official Panzerkampfwagen title, but it would have been called the "Leopard" had it entered production. Its turret design was adopted for the SdKfz 234/2 Puma.

LEGION CONDOR

THE CONDOR Legion (German: Legion Condor) was a unit composed of volunteers from the German Air Force (Luftwaffe) and from the German Army (Wehrmacht Heer) which served with the Nationalists during the Spanish Civil War of July 1936 to March 1939. The Condor Legion developed methods of terror bombing which were used widely in the Second World War shortly afterwards. The bombing of Guernica was the most infamous operation carried out by the Condor Legion during this period. Hugo Sperrle commanded the aircraft units of the Condor Legion and Wilhelm Ritter von Thoma commanded the ground units.

History of military aid to Spain

Following the military coup in Spain at the start of the Spanish Civil War, the Spanish Second Republic turned to the Soviet Union and France for support, and the nationalists requested the support of Hitler's Germany and fascist Italy. The first request for German aircraft was made on 22 July, with an order for 10 transport aircraft. Hitler decided to support the nationalists on 25 or 26 July, but was wary of provoking a Europe-wide war. The Reich Air Travel Ministry concluded that nationalist forces would need at least 20 Ju 52s, flown by Luft Hansa pilots, to carry the Army of Africa from Spanish Morocco to Spain. This mission became known as Operation Magic Fire (German: Feuerzauber). The joint Spanish-German "Spanish-Moroccan Transport Company" (Spanish: Companía Hispano-Marroquí de Transporte, HISMA) and an entirely German company, the Raw Materials and Good Purchasing Company (German: Rohstoffe-

He-111E of the Condor Legion, 1939

und-Waren-Einkaufsgesellschaft, ROWAK) were established. This involvement was kept covert, hidden from both foreign and economic ministries, and funded with three million Reichmarks.

The organisation and recruitment of German volunteers was also kept secret. The first contingent of 86 men left on 1 August, unaware of where they were going. They were accompanied with six biplane fighters, anti-aircraft guns and about 100 tons of other supplies. They were placed at Tablada airfield near Seville, and accompanied by German Air transport began the airlift of Franco's troops to Spain. Germany's involvement grew in September to encompass the Wehrmacht's other branches; Operation Magic Fire was renamed Operation Guido in November. A wide belief was that the soldiers would train Spanish nationalists, and not engage. The head of the Kriegsmarine provided submarines from 24 October. The German navy also provided various surface ships and coordinated movement of German supplies to Spain. German U-Boats were dispatched to Spanish waters under the codename Ursula.

Ju 52 plane undergoing maintenance

In the two weeks following 27 July, German transport moved nearly 2,500 troops of the Army of Africa to Spain. By 11 October, the mission's official end, 13,500 troops, 127 machine guns and 36 field guns had been carried into Spain from Morocco. Over this period there was a movement from training and supply missions of overt combat. The operation leader, Alexander von Scheele, was replaced by Walter Warlimont. In September, 86 tons of bombs, 40 Panzer PzKpfw I tanks and 122 personnel had been landed in Spain; they were accompanied with 108 aircraft in the July–October period, split between aircraft for the Nationalist faction itself and planes for German volunteers in Spain.

German air crews supported the Nationalist advance on Madrid, and the successful relief of the Siege of the Alcázar. Ultimately, this phase of the Siege of Madrid would be unsuccessful. Soviet air support for the Republican was growing, particularly through the supply of Polikarpov aircraft. Warlimont appealed to Nazi Germany to step up support. Following German recognition of Franco's government on 30 September, German efforts in Spain were reorganised and expanded. The existing command structure was replaced with the Winterübung Rügen, and the military units already in Spain were formed into a new legion, which was briefly called the Iron Rations (German: Eiserne Rationen) and the Iron Legion (German: Eiserne Legion) before Göring renamed it the Condor Legion (German: Legion Condor). The first German chargé to Franco's government, General Wilhelm von Faupel, arrived in November, but was told not to interfere in military matters.

Its debut (combat test) was during Spanish Civil War (1936-38). First 32 PzKpfw I along with single Kleiner Panzer Befehlswagen I arrived in October of 1936. Only 106 tanks, (102 Ausf A, Ausf B and 4 Kleiner Panzer Befehlswagen I) saw service with "Condor Legion" (Major Ritter von Thoma's Panzer Abteilung 88 also known as Abteilung Drohne) and General Franco's "Nationalists". Pz.Abt.88 with its 3 companies was based at Cubas near Toledo, where German instructors trained future Spanish crews, while the unit was used for training duties and combat (e.g. assault on Madrid). Panzerkampfwagen I tanks proved to be outclassed by Soviet T-26 and BT-5 provided to "The Republicans".

Some Panzerkampfwagen I captured by "The Republicans" were rearmed with French Hotchkiss 25mm Model 1934 or 1937 anti-tank guns mounted in a modified turret (PzKpfw I Ausf. A mit 20mm Flak L/65 Breda Model 1935). During Spanish Civil

Dornier Do 17 E-1 of the Condor Legion

A back view of a Panzer I from the Condor Legion in Spain.

War, PzKpfw I Ausf B was experimentally armed with Italian 20mm Breda Modello (model) 1935 light anti-aircraft gun mounted in a modified turret, in order to increase its combat potential. Some sources state that three tanks were converted that way.

PzKpfw Is equipped two Nationalist tank battalions (Agrupacion de Carros) - 1st and 2nd Tank Battalion. German High Command used the opportunity of the Spanish Civil War to test their new weapons and tactics of Blitzkrieg. Its very thin armor offered only protection against small firearms and its twin MGs were no match for anything other than infantry units and proved completely useless in combat.

The following information is provided on Gruppe Imker - the codename of the German Ground Contingent of the Condor Legion:

- 1 Pz.Kp (from the 1 Battalion of Panzer Regiment 6 (Neuruppin))
- 2 Pz.Kp.(from the II Battalion of Panzer Regiment 6 (Neuruppin))

- Transport Kp
- Tansport Kp
- Nachrichtenzug (Signals Platoon)
- Werkstatts-Kp (Workshop Company)
- 1 Pak. Kdo. (Antitank Gun Command)

Upon the completion of training, the Spanish tank companies retained their German Pz.Kpfw.1s and accompanied them to the front. The German training companies would then receive another supply of tanks to be used for the next training session. Army ground personnel in Spain never exceeded 600 men at any time. Gruppe Imker (Group Beekeeper) had a staff, under the command of oberstleutnant von Thoma, which coordinated and maintained all direct communications to Germany. Imker's Panzer units were codenamed Gruppe "Drohne" or Group "Drone".

Each company had 11 Pz-Is with 3 companies to a Battalion (Agrupacion) and a T-26 company added later (captured tanks).

Overleaf is a collection of documents to Cpl Eugene Alexejen of Legion Condor, awarded Spanish cross in silver. He was in the Condor Legion with Panzer Regiment 6 "Neuruppin" of the third Panzer Division.

In Spain in early October 1936 General der Panzertruppe Wilhelm Josef Ritter von Thoma was sent by the German high command to Spain as the commander of the group "Imker" (Beekeeper), the ground contingent of the German Condor Legion. Tasked with training Franco's Spanish Nationalist officers and men in tanks, infantry tactics and artillery and signals employment. Cpl Eugene Alexsejen would have been part of this and would have helped in the front line in combat.

Motivation

In the years following the Spanish Civil War, Hitler gave several possible motives for German involvement. Among these were the distraction it provided from German re-militarisation; the

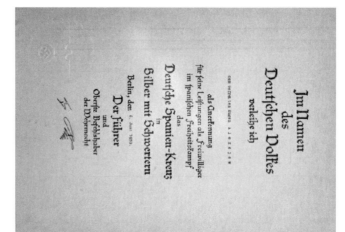

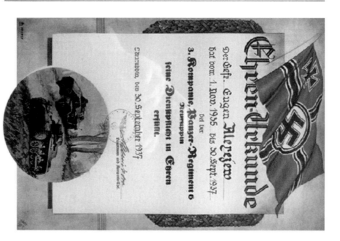

prevention of the spread of communism to Western Europe; the creation of a state friendly to Germany to disrupt Britain and France; and the possibilities for economic expansion. Although the offensive on Madrid was abandoned in March 1937, a series of attacks on weaker Republican-controlled areas was supported by Germany; despite prolonging the Civil War, it would help to distract the other western powers from Hitler's ambitions in central Europe. The offensive on Vizcaya, a mining and industrial centre, would help fuel German industry. On 27 June 1937, Hitler (in a speech at Wurzburg) declared he supported Franco to gain control of Spanish ore.

Discussions over German objectives for intervention occurred in January 1937. Germany was keen to avoid prompting a Europe-wide war, which at the time they felt committing further resources to Spain would do. Contradictory views were held by German officials: Ernst von Weizsäcker suggested it was merely a matter of graceful withdrawal; Hermann Göring stated that Germany would never recognise a "red Spain". A joint Italian–German decision, that the last shipments would be made by the start of February, was agreed.

It has been speculated that Hitler used the Spanish Civil War issue to distract Mussolini from Hitler's own designs on and plans for union (Anschluss) with Austria. The authoritarian Catholic, anti-Nazi Vaterländische Front government of autonomous Austria had been in alliance with Mussolini, and in 1934 the assassination of Austria's authoritarian president Engelbert Dollfuss had already successfully invoked Italian military assistance in case of a German invasion.

A communique in December 1936, from German ambassador in Rome Ulrich von Hassell illustrates another point:

> The role played by the Spanish conflict as regards Italy's relations with France and England could be similar to that of the Abyssinian conflict, bringing out clearly the actual, opposing interests of the powers and thus preventing Italy from being drawn into the net of the Western powers and used for their machinations. All the more clearly will Italy recognize the advisability of confronting the Western powers shoulder to shoulder with Germany.

Operational record

The Condor Legion, upon establishment, consisted of the Kampfgruppe 88, with three squadrons of Ju 52 bombers and the Jagdgruppe 88 with three squadrons of Heinkel He 51 fighters, the reconnaissance Aufklärungsgruppe 88 (supplemented by the Aufklärungsgruppe See 88), an anti-aircraft group, the Flakbteilung 88, and a signals group, the Nachrichtenabteilung 88. Overall command was given to Hugo Sperrle, with Alexander Holle as chief of staff. Scheele was transferred to become a military attaché in Salamanca. Two armoured units under the command of Wilhelm Ritter von Thoma, with four tanks each, were also operational.

The Nationalists were supported by German and Italian units and materials at the Battle of Madrid. However, the military situation in Madrid remained poor for the nationalists, and both German and Italian aircraft (under Franco's direction) began bombing raids on the city as a whole. The Germans were keen to observe the effects of civilian bombings and deliberate burning of the city. Offensives involving German aircraft, as well as the bombings, were unsuccessful. Increasing Republican air superiority became apparent, particularly the strength of the Soviet Polikarpov I-15 and I-16 aircraft. Historian Hugh Thomas describes their armaments as "primitive". Faupel, in November–December, urged the creation of a single German unit of 15,000–30,000, believing it would be enough to turn the tide of the war to the Nationalists. Hans-Heinrich Dieckhoff argued this would insufficient, and that larger measures could provoke the wrath of the Spanish.Between late 1936 and early 1937, new aircraft were sent to the Condor Legion, including Henschel Hs 123 dive bombers, and prototypes of the Heinkel He 112 and Messerschmitt Bf 109, with the last proving the most successful. The Heinkel He 111 was added to the bomber fleet, along with the Dornier Do 17 (E and F types). Older aircraft were passed onto the Nationalists. By the end of 1936, 7,000 Germans were in Spain.

German forces also operated in the Battle of Jarama, which began with a Nationalist offensive on 6 February 1937. It included German-supplied ground forces, including two batteries of machine guns, a tank division, and the Condor Legion's anti-aircraft guns. Bombing by both Republican and Nationalist aircraft, including Ju 52s from the Legion, helped ensure a stalemate. It showed up the inadequacy of the Legion's aircraft, faced with superior Soviet-made fighters. Von Thorma requested Irish nationalist support for a tank advance at one point, never to be replicated. Use of He 51 and Ju 52s, and the Legion's anti-aircraft guns used in ground roles, only partly mitigated what was a significant defeat for the Nationalists at the Battle of Guadalajara during March. A joint Italian-German general had been set up in January 1937 to advise Franco on war planning. The defeat of a significant Italian force and the growing Soviet superiority in tanks and aircraft led the Germans to support a plan to abandon the offensive on Madrid and instead concentrate a series of attacks on weaker Republican-controlled areas. Whilst many countries believed motorised troops to have been proven less effective than first thought, it was the inadequacy of the Italians as a fighting force that dominated German thought.

The Vizcaya Campaign

The isolated area of Vizcaya, a predominantly Basque part of northern Spain, was the most immediate target, in what was called the War in the North. It was largely a Nationalist and Italian offensive, but was supported by a consistently re-equipping Condor Legion. The terrain was favourable, with the planes coming over a range of mountains to the south, masking their entrance. Sperrle remained in Salamanca; Wolfram von Richthofen replaced Holle in January as deputy and in actual command. Since the Basque air force was very limited, even fighters were used in ground-attack roles. The Legion's air force initially attacked the towns of Ochandiano and Durango. Durango had no anti-aircraft defence, and only minor other defences. According to the Basques, 250 civilians died on the 31 March, including the priest, nuns and congregation of a church ceremony. The Germans, with their air raids, were hated. The Basque ground forces were in full retreat towards Bilbao, through the town of Guernica, which was attacked on 26 April in one of the most controversial attacks of the Spanish Civil War.

Guernica

In Operation Rügen, waves of Ju 52 and He 51 planes bombed and strafed targets in Guernica. The number of casualties is a matter of controversy, with perhaps 200–300 people killed; the number reported dead by the Basques was 1,654 dead and 889

Ruins of Guernica (1937)

wounded. Several explanations were put forward by the Nationalists, including blaming the attack on the Republicans, that the attack on the town had been a prolonged offensive, or that the Rentería bridge, outside Guernica, was the true target. However, the nature of the operation itself, including the formation and armaments used, makes this seem unlikely. Guernica was a clear target of the Condor Legion, rather than the Nationalists as a whole. The offensive on Bilbao, when it eventually came on 11 July, was supported by ground units of the Condor Legion, and extensive air operations. It proved the worth of the Condor Legion to the Nationalist cause.

The first English-language media reports of the destruction in Guernica appeared two days later. George Steer, a reporter for The Times, who was covering the Spanish Civil War from inside the country, authored the first full account of events. Steer's reporting set the tone for much of the subsequent reportage. Steer pointed out the clear German complicity in the action. The evidence of three small bomb cases stamped with the German

Imperial Eagle made clear that the official German position of neutrality in the Civil War and the signing of a Non-Intervention Pact was a sham. Steer's report was syndicated to the New York Times and then worldwide, generating widespread shock, outrage, and fear.

Further campaigns

The Condor Legion also took part in the Battle of Brunete, designed as a Republican offensive to take the pressure off northern Spain, where fighting was ongoing. The Legion was sent from the north to reinforce the broken line. There were repeated raids on Republican armoured vehicles and later defensive positions by both bombers and fighters based at Salamanca. Republican aircraft were ineffective, despite Nationalist fears, compared with German aircraft; the Messerschmitt Bf 109 was shown to be superior to the I-15 and I-16 models used by Republican forces. The Legion lost 8 aircraft, but claimed 18 victories. German tactics were also improved with the experience of Brunete, particularly the en masse use of tanks by the Nationalists.

The Nationalists returned to focus on the capture of northern Spain. German test aircraft, with latest models, faced an outdated Basque air force, although it did have some Russian planes. Heavy aerial bombardment from 200 Nationalist, German and Italian planes was used far behind Basque lines in August 1937, leading to the fall of Santander after the Battle of Santander on 1 September. The formal battle in Asturias ended with the fall of Gijón on 21 October. A large amount of ammunitions had been used by the Legion, including a million machine gun rounds and 2,500 tonnes of bombs. Germany immediately began to ship industrial production back to Germany. Sperrle argued repeatedly with Faupel, and against HISMA's monopoly. Faupel was replaced by Franco, through Sperrle. Sperrle also returned to Germany and was replaced by Helmuth Volkmann; following disagreements with Volkmann, Von Richthofen would be replaced with Hermann Plocher in early 1938.

Whilst the next major campaign – Madrid or Barcelona – was discussed, the Condor Legion was moved to Soria and began a week of strikes against Republican airfields, halted by the Republican advance on Teruel and the ensuing Battle of Teruel. Both the Legion's land and air forces were used, and the Legion moved to Bronchales. Poor weather resulted in few flights, and the town fell to Republican forces on 6 January. Up to 100 sorties a day were launched during the Nationalist's counter-offensive through the Alfambra valley. The Junkers Ju 87A was used for the first time on the advance on Teruel, which was retaken on 22 February. The continued Nationalist offensive on Aragon in April–June 1937, including the Battle of Belchite, involved bombing raids and the use of the Legion's ground forces. The Legion was switched to focus in the north, towards the Segre river, before moving south again following Nationalist successes. The Legion moved its main headquarters to Benicarlo; single-engined planes operated from airfields nearby, and twin-engined planes from Zaragoza. Hitler's words to his colleagues belied a change in attitude about the war in Germany – that a quick victory in the war was not desirable, a mere continuation of the war would be preferable. German policy would be to prevent a Republican defeat. However, casualties were beginning to mount for the Legion and, combined with a resurgence in Republican air activity, the Nationalist advance stalled. This was, perhaps, because of the reluctance of commanders in Germany to supply reinforcements, with the Czechoslovakia crisis mounting. Arguments over the bill to the Germans – now rising at 10 million Reichmarks a month – continued, unresolved. The Legion's materiel had been exhausted.

On 24–25 July, Republican forces launched the last major offensive of the war, the Battle of the Ebro. Reconnaissance units of the Condor Legion had noticed a troop build-up, and warned

Nationalists forces. The warning went unheeded. Although the Republic gained ground, Republican forces failed to gain control of Ganesa, with 422 sorties by the Legion (with around 70 aircraft operational) having considerable effect. The rest of the battle saw a series of attacks using artillery or air strikes, followed by a Nationalist ground advance. However, tensions in Czechoslovakia and a shortage of pilots in Germany led to the return of 250 pilots from the Legion, around half of them being bomber crews. Although trained Spaniards made up some of the shortfall, Volkmann complained to central command in Berlin, which would lead to his recall in September. During the battle, which saw 113 days of fighting, only 10 aircraft were lost (some by accident) and 14 were badly damaged; the Legion claimed around 100 Republican aircraft, a third of those lost. Only 5 aircrew had been killed, and 6 captured. Aid from Germany temporarily halted in mid-September. Germany and Nationalist Spain settled the issue of German interests in Spanish mines.

The Legion took a short break from active duty to receive new aircraft, including Bf 109Es, He 111Es and Js, and Hs 126As, bringing its strength to 96 aircraft, around a fifth of the Nationalist's force as a whole. Von Richthofen returned to Spain in overall command, with Hans Seidemann as chief of staff. This reinforcement may have been the single most important intervention by a foreign side in the war, enabling a counterattack after the Battle of the Ebro. It mainly took part in operations against the remaining Republican air force during January–February 1939, with considerable success. After it took part in parades in Barcelona and elsewhere, and minor duties over Madrid, it was rapidly dissolved. The men returned on 26 May; the best aircraft were returned to Germany and the rest of the equipment bought by the new Spanish regime.

The Condor Legion claimed to have destroyed 320 Republican planes using aircraft (either shot down or bombed on the ground), and shot down another 52 using anti-aircraft guns. They also claimed to have destroyed 60 ships. They lost 72 aircraft due to hostile action, and another 160 to accidents.

Maritime operations

The Maritime Reconnaissance Staffel 88 (German: Aufklärungsstaffel See 88) was the Condor Legion's maritime unit under the command of Karl Heinz Wolff. Operating independently of the land-based division, it acted against enemy shipping, ports, coastal communications and occasionally inland targets such as bridges. It used floatplanes, starting with the Heinkel He 60, which began operating at Cadiz in October 1936. Missions started as reconnaissance but, following the move from Cadiz to Mellila in Spanish Morocco in December 1936, the focus shifted to attacks on shipping. It was again moved in February 1937 to Málaga, newly captured, and then to Majorca when Málaga proved unsuitable. Beginning in June, operations were expanded to allow attacks on all Republican ports, so long as no British ships were present. 10 ships were attacked in the second half of 1937; however, the Norwegian torpedoes being used proved ineffective, and strafing or bombing targets was used instead.

The arrival of Martin Harlinghausen (known as "Iron Gustav") saw operations expand, and operations targeted Alicante, Almeria, Barcelona and Cartegena. As naval activity declined, inland targets became more numerous, and night missions began. Activities in support of ground forces became the main focus of the unit until the end of hostilities. Both Wolff and Harlinghausen received the Spanish Cross in Gold with Swords and Diamonds. In total, eleven men were killed in action, and five others died due to accident or illness.

Other operations

Overtly, the Kriegsmarine was part of force enforcing the Non-Intervention Agreement from interfering in the Civil War. However, this agreement was clearly broken by Germany. As a result, the German pocket battleship Deutschland stood guard over Ceuta to prevent interference from Republican ships while Franco transported troops to the Spanish mainland. By mid-October, the German North Sea Group around Spain consisted of the pocket battleships Deutschland and Admiral Scheer, the light cruiser Köln and four torpedo boats. After the Germans claimed that Leipzig had been attacked by an unidentified submarine, it did formally withdraw from international patrols.

Operation Ursula (named after the daughter of Karl Dönitz) saw a group of German U-boats active around Spain. It began on 20 November 1936, with the movement of the U-33 and U-34 from Wilhelmshaven. Any identification marks were obscured, and the whole mission was kept secret. Difficulties in identifying legitimate targets and concerns about discovery limited their operations. During their return to Wilhelmshaven in December, the Republican submarine C-3 was sunk; the Germans claimed this was due to a torpedo fired from U-34, although the Republican's enquiry claimed its loss was due to an internal explosion. Their return marked the official end of Operation Ursula. However, it does seem that further submarines were sent in mid-1937, but details of the operation are not known; six are believed to have been involved.

Abwehr

The German Intelligence service, the Abwehr, working independently of the Legion Condor was secretly involved in Operation Bodden. This was to later play a part in the detection of the Operation Torch invasion fleet.

Military advantages gained

Training

It is known that the leaders of the Army were hesitant about becoming involved in the conflict, and resisted a call made by the Italian government for a dual transfer of ground troops to fight in Spain. The involvement of the Luftwaffe, however, was not entirely restricted and a commonly held viewpoint is that the

"Condor Legion" infantry training school in Ávila, Spain.

involvement of the Luftwaffe in the Civil War constituted a proving ground for troops employed later during World War II. This view is supported by the testimony of Hermann Göring, later Reichsmarschall of the Luftwaffe, when on trial at the International Military Tribunal in Nürnberg. When asked about the decision to use the Luftwaffe, Göring states:

When the Civil War broke out in Spain, Franco sent a call for help to Germany and asked for support, particularly in the air. One should not forget that Franco with his troops was stationed in Africa and that he could not get the troops across, as the fleet was in the hands of the Communists, or, as they called themselves at the time, the competent Revolutionary Government in Spain. The decisive factor was, first of all, to get his troops over to Spain. The Fuehrer thought the matter over. I urged him to give support [to Franco] under all circumstances, firstly, in order to prevent the further spread of communism in that theater and, secondly, to test my young Luftwaffe at this opportunity in this or that technical respect.

This was also a view put forth in western media following

the disengagement of German forces from Spain.

Dozens of Messerschmitt Bf 109 fighters and Heinkel He 111 medium bombers, and from December 1937, at least three Junkers Ju 87 Stuka dive-bombers, first saw active service in the Condor Legion against Soviet-supplied aircraft. The Stuka's first mission flown in Spain was February 1938. Each of these aircraft played a major role during the early years of the Second World War. The Germans also quickly realized that the days of the biplane fighter were finished. The Heinkel He 51 fighter, after suffering many losses during the first 12 months of the conflict, was switched to a ground attack role and later saw service as a trainer.

Other units

The Condor Legion also included non-aircraft units. Panzer crews operating Panzerkampfwagen I light tanks were commanded by Wilhelm Ritter von Thoma. The Germans also tested their 88 mm heavy anti-aircraft artillery which they used to destroy Republican tanks and fortifications using direct fire, as well as enemy aircraft in their designed role.

German involvement in Spain also saw the development of the first air ambulance service for evacuation of wounded combatants.

Technical advances

One important factor in World War II which is thought to have directly resulted from the conflict is the technical development of the Messerschmitt Bf 109. The V3 – V6 types entered service in Spain directly from operational trials around January 1937. In the spring of 1938 these were joined by type C aircraft with type Es being first fielded in December 1938.

As a result of combat in Spain improvements were also made to the 88 mm gun.

Tactics

Alongside the potential for gains in combat experience it is also

Bf 109 C-1, Jagdgruppe 88, Legion Condor

thought that various strategic initiatives were first trialed as part of Luftwaffe involvement in the conflict. Theories on strategic bombing were first developed by the Luftwaffe with the first exhibition of "carpet bombing" in the September 1937 Asturias campaign. As the fighting progressed into March 1938 Italian pilots under Fieldmarshal Hugo Sperrle were involved in thirteen raids against Barcelona involving fire and gas bombs. These particular raids resulted in the deaths of thousands of civilians.[citation needed] It is worth noting that a subsequent commander of the Legion in Spain, Wolfram Freiherr von Richthofen was to become heavily involved in the operation of the Luftwaffe as part of Operation Barbarossa.

Tactics of combined or joint operations were a particular focus. Close air support for Nationalist troops, attack bombing of Republican troop concentrations, and strafing became features of the war. The Legion worked closely in missions which maximized the fighting ability of the Nationalist air force and troops, the Italian CTV, and pilots from the Aviazione Legionaria (Legionary Air Force). German Air ace Adolf Galland was to claim after World War II that although there was a focus on taking lessons from the conflict in Spain, he believed the wrong conclusions were drawn by the German High Command with particular respect to the Luftwaffe:

Whatever may have been the importance of the tests of

German arms in the Spanish Civil War from tactical, technical and operational points of view, they did not provide the experience that was needed nor lead to the formulation of sound strategic concepts.

Reaction to German involvement

Various sympathetic writers participated in condemning the scarcely concealed interference by Germany and Italy. An example was Heinrich Mann, who appealed from exile in France with the slogan "German soldiers! A rogue sends you to Spain!" in response to the Legion's involvement.

Other states tacitly approved the fight of the German Legion against the Soviet-supplied Spanish Republican side.

Treatment in Nazi Germany

As part of his longterm "Blumenkrieg" strategy Hitler drew parallels between the conflict in Spain and the peaceful methods he used to gain control in Germany. The regime also made use of the conflict as an opportunity for political education and aggrandizement. Highlighting of the military aspects and success story for German arms is also evident with the publication of various pulp semi-autobiographical works in 1939, most notably:

- Wir funken für Franco (literally We transmit for Franco) by Hellmut Führing,
- Als Jagdflieger in Spanien (As a fighter pilot in Spain) by Hannes Trautloft,
- Das Buch der Spanienflieger (The Spanish Pilot's Book) by Hauptmann Wulf Bley.

Each book had a high circulation; in the case of Bley the circulation was estimated at over 1 million books sold. Although accurate in part these works are now accepted by scholars on the period and conflict as laced with propaganda which emphasizes daring escapades and fails to address the realities of military combat in general.

CONTEMPORARY DOCUMENTS

"RECONNAISSANCE BY LIGHT TANK PLATOONS"

FROM INTELLIGENCE BULLETIN MAY 1943

1. INTRODUCTION

In German tank organizations, a light tank platoon consisting of seven Pz. Kw. 2's is an organic part both of the regimental headquarters company and the battalion headquarters company. The regimental light tank platoon is normally used for reconnaissance purposes. German doctrine covering the reconnaissance duties of patrols drawn from these platoons is summarized below. (It assumes that superior German forces are conducting an advance.)

2. THE DOCTRINE

a. Teamwork

Teamwork, the Germans point out, is the secret of successful reconnaissance. They believe that haphazardly formed reconnaissance patrols, made up of men who have never worked together before, are of little value.

b. Reconnaissance Before H-Hour

(1) Orders.—Orders given to light tank patrols which are to perform reconnaissance before H-hour include:

    (a) Information about hostile forces and the terrain.

    (b) German intentions (especially those of a patrol's own and flanking units).

(c) Composition of the patrol.

(d) Time of departure.

(e) Line of advance and objectives.

(f) Method and procedure of reporting (radio or motorcycle).

(g) Position of the patrol commander, and of the commander to whom he will report.

(h) Action to be taken on completion of task, or on meeting superior opposing forces.

It is prohibited to take written orders and situation maps on reconnaissance. Special precautions are insisted upon when markings of any kind are made on maps used on reconnaissance; these markings are required to be of a kind which will not reveal German dispositions if the maps are captured.

(2) Information Needed Beforehand.—For its disposition and method of work, the German patrol depends on knowing:

(a) Up to what point contact with the opposition is unlikely. (Until reaching this point, the patrol saves time by advancing rapidly and avoiding elaborate protective measures.)

(b) At what point contact is probable. (After this, increased alertness is maintained.)

(c) At what point contact is certain. (Here the patrol is ready for action.)

The patrol commander is also given necessary particulars regarding air support and information as to the attitude of the civil population.

(3) Method of Advance.—The light tank patrol advances rapidly from one observation point to the next, making use at first of roads and paths, but later, as it approaches hostile forces, using all available cover. When approaching villages, woods, or defiles, the patrol leaves the road in sufficient time to upset the opposition's aimed antitank-fire calculations.

(4) Command.—The German patrol commander makes a rapid estimate of our position, and tries to attack and overrun us if

he thinks that we are weak. If such a move does not seem advisable, he attempts to discover the type and strength of the opposition encountered, without becoming involved in combat.

"Keen, capable, and well-trained officers or noncoms must be selected to command the light tank patrol," the Germans state. "These must be constituted of quick-thinking, resourceful troops who have functioned as a unit long enough to know and have confidence in their leader."

c. Reconnaissance after H-Hour

(1) Mission.—The mission of reconnaissance after H-hour is to explore the hostile position in detail, to protect German deployment, and to discover hostile gun positions, as well as natural and artificial obstacles in the line of advance.

(2) How Performed.—The mission is carried out by light tank patrols (which may be reinforced) operating ahead or on the flanks, as in reconnaissance before H-hour. The reconnaissance tanks employed immediately ahead or to a forward flank are detailed automatically by the first wave of the attacking force. (Normally, one light tank per platoon of heavier tanks in the first wave, and always the same light tank. The remaining light tanks work behind the first wave, performing other duties.) The reconnaissance tanks advance rapidly, making for suitable high ground. They keep 300 to 500 yards ahead of the first wave, and maintain visual contact with it. The reconnaissance tanks observe from open turrets or, if fired on, through their telescopes, with turrets closed. They advance by bounds, from cover to cover, keeping the terrain ahead under continuous observation.

The tanks in the first wave, especially the Pz. Kw. 4's, cover the reconnaissance tanks as they advance.

When the reconnaissance tanks contact our infantry, they attempt to overrun us and, if they are successful, they report and continue their mission. A reconnaissance tank discovering hostile antitank weapons and artillery reports them, takes up a position, and waits for the rest of its company. While waiting, it fires on hostile antitank weapons.

Tanks are avoided, but are observed from concealed positions. The reconnaissance tanks report suitable terrain for meeting an attack by hostile tanks. As under the circumstances described in the previous paragraph, each reconnaissance tank waits for the rest of its company.

Opposition which begins to retreat is promptly attacked, the reconnaissance tanks reporting the development and continuing the pursuit.

In the event of an attack by the opposition, the reconnaissance tanks take up a position, meet the attack, report, and wait for the rest of their companies to come up.

In all these instances, the reconnaissance tanks avoid obstructing the field of fire of the heavier tanks following them. Throughout, the light tanks report by radio if it is available, by prearranged flag or smoke signals, or by significant firing or maneuvering.

PZ. JÄG. II AUS D, E FÜR 7.62 CM PAK 36 (SD. KFZ. 131): S.P. ANTITANK GUN (RUSSIAN)

CATALOG OF ENEMY ORDNANCE ORIGINALLY PUBLISHED BY U.S. OFFICE OF CHIEF OF ORDNANCE, 1945

The Pz. Kpfw. II chassis embodying the suspension on four large bogie wheels has been used as a self-propelled mount for the German modified Russian gun 7.62 cm Pak 36 (r) as well as the Pz. Kpfw. II models utilizing five bogie wheels. These equipments are used in an antitank capacity.

The turret and superstructure of the original tank has been removed and replaced by a high box-like superstructure shield of approximately 15 mm thickness, sloping about 75° to the horizontal. Centrally located above the lower shield superstructure is a three-sided shield of approximately 10 mm thickness with a slotted front plate through which the long muzzle of the gun projects well over the front of the chassis. The original shield of the gun has been retained.

The gun, 163 1/2 inches in length including the muzzle brake, is of monobloc construction. The breech mechanism is of the falling-wedge type. The elevating gear is operated by a handwheel located on the left side of the gun; the traversing gear is on the right. The estimated elevation of the piece is -5° to +22°; traverse 65°. Its muzzle velocities are as follows: H.E. shell, 1805 f/s; A.P.C. shell, 2430 f/s. Firing A.P.C. shell this gun will defeat 3.2 inches of homogeneous armor of 30° obliquity at 1000 yards, and 4.1 inches at normal.

SPECIFICATIONS

- Weight: 10.5 tons
- Length: 16 ft. (excl. gun)
- Width: 7 ft., 6 ins.
- Height: 6 ft., 9 ins.
- Ground clearance: 12 ins.
- Tread centers: 5 ft., 10 ins.
- Ground contact: 7 ft., 10 ins.
- Width of track
- Track links: 96 (est.)
- Pitch of track: Fording depth: 3 ft.
- Theoretical radius of action: Roads: 115 miles, Cross-country: 75 miles
- Speed: Roads: 28 m.p.h., Cross-country: 12 m.p.h.
- Armor: Front plate: 30 mm, Sides: 15 mm, Shield: 15 mm
- Armament: 7.62 cm Pak 36 (r)
- Ammunition:—
- Wt. of Projectiles: A.P.C.: 16.7 lb., H.E.: 12.6 lb.
- Engine: Maybach, 140 B.H.P.
- Transmission: 5 speeds forward, 1 reverse
- Steering: Epicyclic clutch brake
- Crew: 4 (probably)

GW. II FÜR 15 CM S.I.G. 33: S.P. HEAVY INFANTRY HOWITZER

CATALOG OF ENEMY ORDNANCE
ORIGINALLY PUBLISHED BY
U.S. OFFICE OF CHIEF OF ORDNANCE, 1945

This vehicle consists of the 15 cm. heavy infantry howitzer mounted in the hull of a modified, turretless Pz. Kpfw. II chassis. The chassis is approximately three feet longer than that of the standard Pz Kw II tank and has six bogie wheels instead of the usual five. The sprockets, rear idlers, bogie wheels, return rollers, steering assembly, gear box and hull nose are those of the Pz. Kpfw. II; the instrument panel is that of a Pz. Kpfw. III. The front shield is in one piece extending straight across the full width of the superstructure. The driver's visor is of the double shutter type. The road performance of this equipment approximates that of the Pz. Kpfw. II tank. The gun, a standard infantry support weapon, is mounted low in the hull, projecting through a vertical slot in the shield. The gun shield is 15 mm thick and is of shallow construction. It extends about a third of the distance of the superstructure to the rear. Unlike the "Wasp" there are no protecting side plates along the entire length of the superstructure.

The gun is 64.57 inches in length, has a muzzle velocity of 790 f.s. and a maximum effective range of 5140 yards. The casting containing the recuperator and buffer, housed underneath the barrel, extends almost to the end of the barrel. The breech mechanism is similar to the 10.5 cm. I.F.H. 18. The elevating qear is operated from the right and the traversing gear from the left. In field mounting its traverse is 11°, its elevation 0° to +73°.

Two types of ammunition are fired, the 15 cm. I. Gr. 33 and the 15 cm. I. Gr. 38. The H.E. capacity is high, 21.8%. The only other shell that the weapon is known to fire is a smoke shell, the 15 cm. I. Gr. 38 Nb. The same percussion fuze, s. I. Gr. Z. 23, which weighs 75 lbs., is used in each case.

SPECIFICATIONS
- Weight: (approx.) 12 tons
- Length: (approx.) 18 ft.
- Width: 7 ft., 4 ins.
- Height (approx.): 5 ft., 6 ins.
- Ground clearance: 13 ins.
- Tread centers: 6 ft., 2 ins.
- Ground contact: Width of track: 11 1/8 ins.,
- Pitch of track: 3 5/8 ins.
- Track links
- Fording depth: 3 ft.
- Theoretical radius of action: Roads: 118 miles, Cross-country: 78 miles
- Speed: Roads: 25 m.p.h., Cross-country: 15 m.p.h.
- Armor: Front plate: 15 + 20 mm, Sides: 15 mm
- Gun shield: 15 mm
- Armament: 15 cm. s.I.G. 33
- Ammunition (rds.)
- Engine: 140 B.H.P. Maybach, HL 62 TRM
- Transmission: 6 forward speeds, 1 reverse
- Steering: Epicyclic clutch brake
- Crew: Probably 4

GW. II (WESPE) FÜR 10.5 CM LE. F. H. 18/2 (SD. KFZ. 124): S.P. LIGHT HOWITZER (WASP)

CATALOG OF ENEMY ORDNANCE ORIGINALLY PUBLISHED BY U.S. OFFICE OF CHIEF OF ORDNANCE, 1945

This equipment, known as the "Wasp," consists of the 10.5 cm. light field howitzer mounted on a chassis which, with the exception that there are only three return rollers, is that of a normal Pz. Kpfw. II tank, Models A-C, with five bogie wheels. Its road performance approximates that of the Pz. Kpfw. II tank.

The gun is the 10.5 cm. 1.F.H. 18 M with muzzle brake. It is mounted at the rear of the chassis within an open top box type shield which is 10 mm thick, its muzzle brake being almost flush with the front of the chassis. Its recuperator and buffer mechanisms, mounted on the bottom and top of the barrel, respectively, are clearly visible beyond the shield. Overlapping the gun shield and sloping back to the rear of the superstructure are side plates, also 10 mm thick. The fighting compartment is open at the top and rear. Its silhouette is high.

The piece has a normal-charge muzzle velocity of 1542 f.s. and a maximum range of 11,650 yards. Firing the long range charge (Fern-ladung) the gun has a muzzle velocity of 1772 f.s. and a maximum range of 13,500 yards. All charges, except the long range, can be fired without the muzzle brake. It has a traverse of 32° and an elevation of -5° to +42°. It is reported to fire four types of ammunition, the 32.6 lb. HE (F. H. Gr.—Feldhaubitze Granate—field howitzer shell), the cast steel HE (F. H. Gr. Stg.—Stahlring—steelring), the 25.9 lb. hollow charge (10 cm. Gr. 39 rot Rohl Ladung—red hollow charge), and a 32.5 lb. smoke shell.

SPECIFICATIONS

- Weight: 12 tons
- Length: 15 ft., 9 ins.
- Width: 7 ft., 4 ins.
- Height: 7 ft., 10 1/2 ins.
- Ground clearance: 13 ins.
- Tread centers: 6 ft., 2 ins.
- Ground contact: 7 ft., 10 ins.
- Width of track: 11 1/8 ins.
- Pitch of track: 3 5/8 ins.
- Track links
- Fording depth: 3 ft.
- Theoretical radius of action: Roads: 125 miles, Cross-country: 70 miles
- Speed: Roads: 24 m.p.h., Cross-country: —
- Armor: Front plate: —, Sides: —
- Armament: 10.5 cm. l.F.H. 18 (M)
- Ammunition (rds.): —
- Engine: Maybach HL 62 TR, 140 h.p.
- Transmission: 6 speeds forward, 1 reverse
- Steering: Epicyclic clutch brake
- Crew: —

PZ. KPFW. II AUS. F (SD. KFZ. 121): LIGHT TANKS

CATALOG OF ENEMY ORDNANCE ORIGINALLY PUBLISHED BY U.S. OFFICE OF CHIEF OF ORDNANCE, 1945

Produced in 1941. This is the latest type of Pz. Kpfw. II tank identified in action. The major modifications appearing in this model are (1) increased thickness of the basic frontal armor, (2) new design of hull nose, (3) use of uninterrupted length of plate for front vertical superstructure plate, (4) use of dummy visor mounted alongside the driver's visor.

The single skin nose of the Model F hull is constructed, of flat plates 35 mm thick with a Brinell hardness of 426 and is nearer vertical than the superimposed nose plate in the earlier reinforced models. This modification to the nose of the hull has shortened its length by approximately five inches.

The turret front and mantlet remain unaltered except for the omission of the additional plates and a corresponding thickening of the basic armor to 30 mm. Model F is equipped with a new driver's visor of the double shutter type. A dummy visor, a one-piece aluminum casting, is mounted alongside the driver's visor on the right, presumably to draw fire from the latter.

The suspension arrangement of five bogie wheels and four return rollers is the same as that utilized in the previous models A, B and C. The power plant consists of the HL 62 TR Maybach, a 6-cylinder, water-cooled gasoline engine rating 140 B.H.P. at 2600 r.p.m.

The transmission is of normal synchromesh, manual control type, providing six forward speeds and one reverse, and the steering system utilizes the epicyclic clutch and brake principle.

Armament comprises one 2.0 cm KwK 30 gun with coaxial 7.92 M.G. 34 in turret.

Models G and J have been mentioned in an official German document but there are no details available.

SPECIFICATIONS

- Weight: 10.5 tons
- Length: 14 ft., 9 ins.
- Width: 7 ft., 4 ins.
- Height: 6 ft., 6 ins.
- Ground clearance: 13 ins.
- Tread centers: 6 ft., 2 ins.
- Ground contact: 7 ft., 10 ins.
- Width of track: 11 1/8 ins.
- Pitch of track: 3 5/8 ins.
- Track links: 106
- Fording depth: 3 ft.
- Theoretical radius of action: Roads: 125 miles, Cross-country: 85 miles
- Speed: Roads: 30 m.p.h., Cross-country: 15 m.p.h.
- Armor: Front plate: 35 mm, Sides: 20 mm
- Armament: One 2.0 cm KwK 30, One 7.92 mm M.G. 34
- Ammunition (rds.): 2 cm gun 180 M.G. 2550
- Engine: 140 B.H.P. Maybach HL 62 TRM
- Transmission: 6 forward speeds, 1 reverse
- Steering: Epicyclic clutch brake
- Crew: 3

PZ. KPFW. II (F) (SD. KFZ. 122): FLAMETHROWER TANK

CATALOG OF ENEMY ORDNANCE ORIGINALLY PUBLISHED BY U.S. OFFICE OF CHIEF OF ORDNANCE, 1945

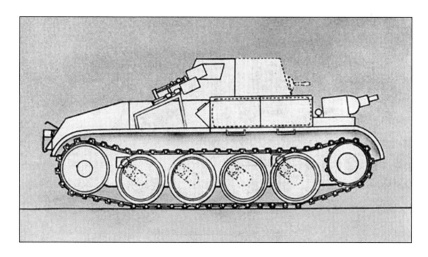

The flamethrower tank, Pz. Kpfw. II (F) is a conversion of Pz. Kpfw. II, Models D and E, which employed the four bogie wheel suspension, and should not be confused with the Model F, which utilizes the five bogie wheel type of suspension. The road performance of the flamethrower tank approximates that of Models D and E.

The flamethrower projectors, having a range of about 35 yards, are mounted in small turrets set well forward on each trackguard. The turrets have 180° traverse while the projectors themselves have a limited elevation. Fuel is supplied from two tanks, provided with armored shields, which are mounted externally on the trackguards, and by compressed nitrogen from the four nitrogen cylinders located inside, below the turret. The tanks have a capacity of 35 gals. each. Two small cylinders mounted just behind the projector turrets contain acetylene, which is used for fuel ignition. The flamethrower is controlled electrically from panels in the turret.

Since this equipment is essentially a close-combat weapon, the tank is liberally fitted for smoke production to screen its movements. Not only is the normal smoke generator rack fitted at the rear, but there is on each trackguard a triple smoke generator discharger, aimed to fire forward, and bowden cable controlled from the turret. Armament also includes a machine gun on a ball mounting in the turret.

SPECIFICATIONS

- Weight: 11 tons
- Length: 16 ft.
- Width: 7 ft., 6 ins.
- Height: 6 ft., 9 ins.
- Ground clearance: 12 ins.
- Tread centers: 5 ft., 10 ins.
- Ground contact: 7 ft., 10 ins.
- Width of track: 11 1/8 ins.
- Pitch of track: 6 3/4 ins.
- Track links: 55
- Fording depth: 3 ft.
- Theoretical radius of action: Roads: 125 miles, Cross-country: 85 miles
- Speed: Roads: 30 m.p.h., Cross-country: 12 m.p.h.
- Armor: Front plate: 30 mm, Sides: 15 mm
- Armament: Two independent flamethrowers, One M.G.
- Ammunition: Flamethrower—70 gals., M.G. 1800 rds.
- Engine: 140 B.H.P. Maybach, HL 62 TRM
- Transmission: 6 speeds forward, 1 reverse
- Steering: Epicyclic clutch brake
- Crew: 3

PZ. KPFW. II AUS D, E (SD. KFZ. 121): LIGHT TANKS

CATALOG OF ENEMY ORDNANCE ORIGINALLY PUBLISHED BY U.S. OFFICE OF CHIEF OF ORDNANCE, 1945

Produced in 1939. Comparatively few of these models were made and these were later converted to flamethrower tanks (Pz. Kpfw. II, Aus. (F)).

Model D—Although the hull, turret, and superstructure of this model are similar to preceding models, its suspension arrangement of four large, rubber-tired, Christie-type bogie wheels which touch the top and bottom of the track make it easy to recognize. Models D and E are the only Pz. Kpfw. II tanks with this type of suspension. The bogie wheels are large enough to eliminate return rollers. The front drive sprocket, rear idler, and the dry-pin, center-guide track complete the suspension assembly. The track can be fitted with snow spuds. These are inserted in the outer web members and held by a split cotter-pin.

The power plant is the Maybach HL 62 TR, six-cylinder, water-cooled engine rated at 140 B.H.P. The transmission provides five forward speeds and one reverse. The steering system embodies the epicyclic clutch and brake principle.

The normal Pz. Kpfw. II armament of one 2 cm Kw.K. 30 with one coaxial 7.92 mm M.G. 34 is mounted. Armor plate thicknesses range from 30 mm front to 15 mm sides.

Model E—Same as Model D.

SPECIFICATIONS

- Weight: 10 tons
- Length: 16 ft.
- Width: 7 ft., 6 ins.
- Height: 6 ft., 9 ins.
- Ground clearance: 12 ins.
- Tread centers: 5 ft., 10 ins.
- Ground contact: 7 ft., 10 ins.
- Width of track:—
- Pitch of track:—
- Track links: 96 (est.)
- Fording depth: 3 ft.
- Theoretical radius of action, Roads: 125 miles, Cross-country: 85 miles
- Speed: Roads: 30 m.p.h., Cross-country: 12 m.p.h.
- Armor: Front plate: 30 mm, Sides: 15 mm
- Armament: 1—2.0 cm Kw.K. 30, 1—7.92 M.G. 34
- Ammunition:—
- Engine: Maybach 140 B.H.P.
- Transmission: Synchromesh, 5 speeds forward, 1 reverse
- Steering: Epicyclic clutch brake
- Crew: 3

PZ. KPFW. II AUS A, B, C (SD. KFZ. 121): LIGHT TANKS

CATALOG OF ENEMY ORDNANCE ORIGINALLY PUBLISHED BY U.S. OFFICE OF CHIEF OF ORDNANCE, 1945

Model A was produced in 1937, followed by B and C in 1938. It is not known whether there are any important differences between these models. All had a suspension consisting of five equally spaced rubber-tired bogie wheels on each side mounted independently on suspension arms pivoted on hull and provided with quarter elliptic leaf springs. There are four 8½ in. diameter return rollers on each side, a 2 ft., 7 in. diameter sprocket, and a 2 ft., 1 in. diameter idler.

The frontal armor of this series was originally only 15 mm thick and the hull had a rounded nose formed by the bending of a single plate which also incorporated the glacis and nose plate. At some time after the battle of France (1940) the armor of these models was reinforced by bolting 20 mm armor plates on the front of the tank. The additional armor on the front of the hull consisted of flat nose and glacis plates which entirely altered the appearance of the hull and nose and gave the effect of spaced armor in front of the rounded part of the basic plate. The gun mantlet armor was thickened by the addition of a 15 mm plate.

The Maybach, HL 62 TR, 6-cylinder gasoline engine, which comprises the power plant, has a rating of 140 h.p.

The armament consists of a 2.0 cm gun which is fired by a trigger on the elevating handwheel, and a coaxial 7.92 mm M.G. 34 which is fired by a trigger on the traversing handwheel.

These models are often converted for use as mounts for heavy anti-tank guns such as the 7.5 cm Pak 40 and the 7.62 cm Pak 36 (r), as well as the 10.5 cm l.F.H. 18 M, known as the Wasp, and the 15 cm s.I.G. 33; the suspension for the latter having a sixth bogie wheel.

SPECIFICATIONS

- Weight: 10 tons
- Length: 15 ft., 2 3/4 ins.
- Width (overall): 7 ft., 4 ins.
- Height: 6 ft., 5 3/4 ins.
- Ground clearance: 13 ins.
- Tread centers: 6 ft., 2 ins.
- Ground contact: 7 ft., 10 ins.
- Width of track: 11 1/8 ins.
- Pitch of track: 3 5/8 ins.
- Track links: 105
- Fording depth: 3 ft.
- Theoretical radius of action: Roads: 125 miles, Cross-country: 85 miles
- Speed: Roads: 30 m.p.h., Cross-country: 15 m.p.h.
- Armor: Front plate: 15 + 20 mm, Sides: 15 mm
- Armament: One 2.0 cm KwK 30, One 7.92 mm M.G. 34
- Ammunition: 2.0 cm gun 180, M.G. 1425
- Engine: 140 h.p. Maybach HL 62 TRM
- Transmission: Crash-type gear box, 6 fwd. speeds, 1 reverse
- Steering: Epicyclic clutch brake
- Crew: 3

PZ. KPFW. II AUS A1, A2, A3, B, C: LIGHT TANKS

CATALOG OF ENEMY ORDNANCE
ORIGINALLY PUBLISHED BY
U.S. OFFICE OF CHIEF OF ORDNANCE, 1945

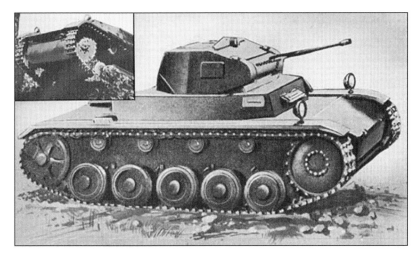

The early development of the Pz. Kpfw. II is indicated by five models, a1, a2, a3, b and c. They were considered as prototype tanks.

Model a1—Had a suspension arrangement of six small bogie wheels, each side mounted on three hull pivots connected by an outside girder. There were four return rollers, sprocket, and a cast rear idler. It weighed about 8.4 tons, was manned by a crew of three and mounted one 2 cm KwK 30 and a coaxial 7.92 mm M.G. 34 in the turret. It was powered by a six-cylinder Maybach (HL 57 TR) gasoline engine and was fitted with epicyclic and brake steering without a final reduction gear. The frontal armor was 20 mm in thickness, the sides 15 mm.

Model a2—Same as Model a1 except for variation in construction of engine compartment and welded rear idler instead of cast.

Model a3—Same as Model a1 except for minor modifications in the suspension arrangement and cooling system.

Model b—Incorporated an improved Maybach (HL 62 TR) engine, as well as a new track with wider driving sprockets, bogie wheels and return rollers. A final reduction gear was also introduced, which necessitated slight alterations in the structure of the front of the hull. The model weighed 9 tons.

Model c—An entirely new suspension comprising five independently sprung bogie wheels on each side made its appearance in this model. It is believed that the torsion bar system of bogie wheel suspension originated in this tank. Modifications to the driving sprocket, rear idler, and return rollers, the latter of which now numbered four, were made. Improved epicyclic and steering brakes were also introduced, the latter being equipped with automatic take-up to compensate for wear. Model c weighed 9 1/2 tons.

SPECIFICATIONS
- Weight: 8 1/2 to 9 1/2 tons
- Length: 15 ft., 2 ins.
- Width: 7 ft., 4 ins.
- Height: 6 ft., 5 ins.
- Ground clearance: 13 ins.
- Tread centers: 6 ft., 2 ins.
- Ground contact: 7 ft., 10 ins.
- Width of track: 11 1/8 ins.
- Pitch of rack: 3 5/8 ins.
- Track links: 106
- Fording depth: 3 ft.
- Theoretical radius of action: Roads: 102 miles, Cross-country: 60 miles
- Speed: Roads: 30 m.p.h., Cross-country: 15 m.p.h.
- Armor: Front plate: 20 mm, Sides: 15 mm
- Armament: One 2 cm KwK 30, One M.G. 34

- Ammunition (rds.): 2 cm gun 180, M.G. 2550
- Engine: HL 57 TR or HL TRM 62
- Maybach: 140 B.H.P.
- Transmission: 6 speeds forward, 1 reverse
- Steering: Epicyclic clutch brake
- Crew: 3

PZ. JÄG. II AUS. A-E U.F FÜR 7.5 CM PAK 40 (SD. KFZ. 131): S.P. ANTITANK GUN

CATALOG OF ENEMY ORDNANCE ORIGINALLY PUBLISHED BY U.S. OFFICE OF CHIEF OF ORDNANCE, 1945

Produced in 1942. This antitank equipment was encountered in the battle of Tunisia. It is composed of the 7.5 cm antitank gun mounted on a Pz. Kpfw. II chassis and its road performance will closely follow that of the Pz. Kpfw. II tank.

The gun, which retains its original shield, recoil system, traversing and elevating gears, is mounted on a platform high on the hull and fires forward. A protective shield 10 mm thick, which slopes away to the rear of the chassis, has been provided. The shield is nearly rectangular except for a projecting portion in front of the gun mounting itself and the top and back are apparently open. The traverse of the gun is limited due to the gun shield fouling the protective shield. A barrel support for travelling is fitted in front of the hull.

The piece, 134 inches in length, is a monobloc type, semi-automatic, with horizontal sliding breech. It consists of barrel with shoes; breech ring with locking ring; breech block with firing mechanism; semi-automatic gear and muzzle brake. The recoil mechanism is comprised of a buffer cylinder, filled with a mixture of glycerine and distilled water, mounted in the cradle and secured by a nut to the front end plate. The piston rod, which is connected to the gun lug, is hollow, and is fitted with a bronze piston head. Ports are drilled in the conical part of the piston. A tapered rod is screwed into the front plug of the cylinder and projects into the hollow piston rod. During recoil the piston moves to the rear and the oil is forced from the buffer cylinder through the ports in the piston and hence through the annular space between the tapered rod and a bushing fitted in the piston. Recoil control is effected by a brass control plunger screwed to the end of the tapered rod. The recuperator is hydro-pneumatic.

SPECIFICATIONS

- Weight: 10 tons
- Length: 15 ft., 2¾ ins.
- Width: 7 ft., 4 ins.
- Height: 6 ft., 5¾ ins.
- Ground clearance: 13 ins.
- Tread centers: 6 ft., 2 ins.
- Ground contact: 7 ft., 10 ins.
- Width of track: 11 1/8 ins.
- Pitch of track: 3 5/8 ins.
- Track links: 105
- Fording depth: 3 ft.
- Theoretical radius of action: Roads: 118 miles, Cross-country: 78 miles
- Speed: Roads: 25 m.p.h., Cross-country: 12 m.p.h.
- Armor: Front plate: 15 + 20 mm, Sides: 15 mm
- Armament: 7.5 cm Pak 40 A.T. gun.
- Max. effective range: 3200 yards. M.V. (Wt. 12.6 lb.): H.E.

1800 f.s. M.V. (Wt. 15 lb.): A.P.C. 2525 f.s.
- Elevation: -5° to +22°. Traverse: 65°: :
- Penetration of homogeneous armor—A.P.C.B.C. shell
  500 yds.: 4.0″ at 30°, 4.8″ normal
  1000 yds.: 3.6″ at 30°, 4.3″ normal
  1500 yds.: 3.2″ at 30°, 3.9″ normal
  2000 yds.: 2.8″ at 30°, 3.4″ normal
  2500 yds.: 2.5″ at 30°, 3.0″ normal
- Ammunition:—
- Engine: Maybach HL 62 TRM, 140 h.p.
- Transmission: Crash-type gear box, 6 fwd. speeds, 1 reverse
- Steering: Epicyclic clutch brake
- Crew: Probably 4

More from the same series

Most books from the 'Hitler's War Machine' series are edited and endorsed by Emmy Award winning film maker and military historian Bob Carruthers, producer of Discovery Channel's Line of Fire and Weapons of War and BBC's Both Sides of the Line. Long experience and strong editorial control gives the military history enthusiast the ability to buy with confidence.

Tiger I in Combat

Tiger I Crew Manual

Panzers at War 1939-1942

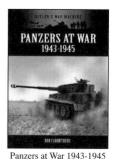
Panzers at War 1943-1945

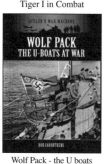
Wolf Pack - the U boats

Poland 1939

Luftwaffe Combat Reports

Sturmgeschütze

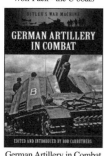
German Artillery in Combat

Panzer Combat Reports

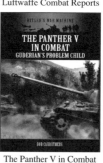
The Panther V in Combat

German Tank Hunters

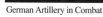
The Afrika Korps in Combat

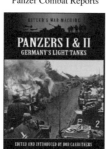

Panzers I & II

Panzer III

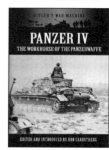
Panzer IV

For more information visit www.pen-and-sword.co.uk